Lecture Notes of the Institute for Computer Sciences, Social Informatics and Telecommunications Engineering 215

More information about this series at http://www.springer.com/series/8197

Yoram Chisik · Jussi Holopainen
Rilla Khaled · José Luis Silva
Paula Alexandra Silva (Eds.)

Intelligent Technologies for Interactive Entertainment

9th International Conference, INTETAIN 2017
Funchal, Portugal, June 20–22, 2017
Proceedings

 Springer

Editors
Yoram Chisik
Madeira Interactive Technologies Institute
Funchal
Portugal

Jussi Holopainen
School of Computer Science
University of Lincoln
Lincoln
UK

Rilla Khaled
Concordia University
Montreal, QC
Canada

José Luis Silva
University Institute of Lisbon
Lisbon
Portugal

Paula Alexandra Silva
National University of Ireland
Maynooth
Ireland

ISSN 1867-8211 ISSN 1867-822X (electronic)
Lecture Notes of the Institute for Computer Sciences, Social Informatics
and Telecommunications Engineering
ISBN 978-3-319-73061-5 ISBN 978-3-319-73062-2 (eBook)
https://doi.org/10.1007/978-3-319-73062-2

Library of Congress Control Number: 2017962879

Printed on acid-free paper

This Springer imprint is published by Springer Nature
The registered company is Springer International Publishing AG
The registered company address is: Gewerbestrasse 11, 6330 Cham, Switzerland

Preface

When Anton Nijholt asked me to chair the 2017 edition of Intetain I liked the idea of holding a small conference on a small island as the ocean affords plenty of room for big ideas to grow. Intetain is a celebration of the future of interactive entertainment. We invited researchers to submit contributions around developments and insights in art, design, science, and engineering regarding novel entertainment-focused devices, paradigms, reconceptualizations, and reconfigurations of entertainment experiences and we were not disappointed, as the submissions although low in number were high in content and concepts crossing the full range of interactive entertainment from physical play to virtual reality and from digital storytelling to email, or are they one and the same?

In *Computer Lib/Dream Machines*, Ted Nelson wrote that "everything is deeply intertwingled" and digital technologies have very deeply intertwingled into the very fabric of our everyday existence with the past distinction between private and public spaces, fact and fiction, tangible and intangible getting more and more blurry by the day. Advances in sensors, actuators, and displays have enabled us to develop new interactive surfaces and new forms of display. While in the past certain objects or locales, be they cave walls, theater stages, cinema screens, statues, or radio receivers, acted as focal points with limited interactivity, now almost any surface can become an interactive device responding to direct and indirect interactions and/or environmental stimuli. Furthermore, we are no longer just looking at screens, they are looking back at us, this has many opportunities but also dangers such as predatory media or predatory state agencies and one of the main challenges for us is to understand how to use this technology as a force for good and how to enable people to counter and control the potential harmful and dangerous aspects of this technological evolution.

Our vision of Intetain is that of a catalyst, a convivial environment for the sharing and germination of ideas and it is our hope that the set of papers presented in this volume will act as a spark for further thought and deliberation long after the sounds emanating from the conference hall have quieted down.

December 2017   Yoram Chisik

Organization

Steering Committee

Imrich Chlamtac   Create-Net, Italy
Anton Nijholt   University of Twente, The Netherlands
     and Imagineering Institute, Malaysia
Antonio Camurri   University of Genoa, Italy

Organizing Committee

General Chair

Yoram Chisik   M-ITI, Madeira Interactive Technologies Institute,
     Portugal

Program Chairs

Rilla Khaled   Concordia University, Canada
Jussi Holopainen   University of Lincoln, UK

Workshops Chairs

Paula Alexandra Silva   Maynooth University, Ireland
Anton Nijholt   University of Twente, The Netherlands
     and Imagineering Institute, Malaysia

Web, Publicity and Social Media Chair

Luis Ferreira   M-ITI, Madeira Interactive Technologies Institute,
     Portugal

Publications Chair

Jose Luis Silva   ISCTE – University Institute of Lisbon, Portugal

Local Arrangements Chair

Ana Lúcia dos Santos Faria   University of Coimbra and M-ITI, Madeira
     Interactive Technologies Institute, Portugal

Conference Manager

Dominika Belisová   EAI, European Alliance for Innovation

Technical Program Committee

Anton Nijholt	University of Twente, The Netherlands
	and Imagineering Institute, Malaysia
Clara Mancini	Open University, UK
Dennis Reidsma	University of Twente, The Netherlands
Lindsay Grace	American University, USA
Regina Bernhaupt	Institut de Recherche en Informatique
	de Toulouse (IRIT), France
Sergi Bermúdez	University of Madeira and Madeira Interactive
	Technologies Institute (M-ITI), Portugal
Staffan Björk	University of Gothenburg, Sweden
Teresa Romão	Universidade NOVA de Lisboa, Portugal
Wolmet Barendregt	University of Gothenburg, Sweden

Reviewers

A. Augusto Sousa	University of Porto, Portugal
A. Eduardo Dias	Universidade Nova de Lisboa, Portugal
Albert Ali Salah	Boğaziçi University, Turkey
Alejandro Catala	University of Twente, The Netherlands
Alexander Muir	Ammachi Labs, Amrita University, India
Anna Zamansky	University of Haifa, Israel
Bill Rogers	The University of Waikato, New Zealand
Carlos Martinho	Instituto Superior Técnico, University of Lisbon,
	Portugal
Chris Geiger	University of Applied Sciences Düsseldorf, Germany
Cristina Sylla	University of Minho, Portugal
Daniel Fabry	Joanneum University of Applied Sciences, Austria
Daniel Fitton	University of Central Lancashire, UK
Elena Márquez Segura	University of California Santa Cruz, USA
Emma Zhang	City University London,
	UK and Imagineering Institute, Malaysia
Eva Cerezo	University of Zaragoza, Spain
Fabrizio Lamberti	Politecnico di Torino, Italy
Fabrizio Valpreda	Politecnico di Torino, Italy
Gavin Sim	University of Central Lancashire, UK
Gilang Andi Pradana	City University London, UK and Imagineering
	Institute, Malaysia
Helmut Hlavacs	University of Vienna, Austria
Ido Iurgel	Rhine-Waal University of Applied Science, Germany
Ilyena Hirskyj-Douglas	University of Central Lancashire, UK
James Manning	Royal Melbourne Institute of Technology (RMIT),
	Australia
Javier Jaen	Politechnical University of Valencia, Spain
Jerry Fails	Boise State University, USA

Contents

Player Expectations of Animal Incorporated Computer Games

Wim van Eck[1,2(✉)] and Maarten H. Lamers[1]

[1] Media Technology Research Group, Leiden Institute of Advanced Computer Science, Leiden University, Leiden, The Netherlands
{w.j.o.m.van.eck,m.h.lamers}@liacs.leidenuniv.nl
[2] Royal Academy of Art, The Hague, The Netherlands

Abstract. Animal incorporated games were both hypothesized and shown to serve multiple desired objectives, among which improvement of animal welfare, strengthening pet-owner relations, and creating new experiences for human players. We study the expected player experience of animal incorporated games through the use of an extended survey ($n = 177$). Our results indicate that respondents expect (a) added unpredictability caused by animal-opponent behavior, (b) increased enjoyment when playing against animals, for a limited duration of time, and (c) that hypothetical exact simulation of animal behavior offers equally interesting opponent behavior. Furthermore, concerns of animal welfare significantly moderate the preference for computer-, exact simulated- or animal-opponents. These outcomes can be used to correct for aspects such as novelty bias, when measuring player experiences in animal incorporated type games.

Keywords: Animal-Computer Interaction · Computer games
Animal welfare · Player expectations

1 Introduction

While computer games are traditionally played against a computer or human opponent(s), either offline or over the internet, there is a recent interest in computer games which incorporate living non-human organisms. Although this is a relatively new topic, there is already quite a variety in intents and approaches towards such games. Some are developed solely for academic purposes [1] while others are commercially available [2] or artistic endeavors [3]. Some are developed for battling animal stress [4] while others incorporate living organisms for behavioral [5] or content generation [6]. Often these games receive notable media attention and since most of them are neither technically nor visually noteworthy, it seems that the inclusion of a living organism is responsible for the expressed interest.

As of yet there has been no empirical study that verifies if the addition of a non-human organism within a computer game indeed raises interest, and if so, why this is the case. By means of a survey we study people's expectations of a game which incorporates living organisms. We hope that the results of this study will give us a better understanding if these types of games are likely to stay compelling or if the

© ICST Institute for Computer Sciences, Social Informatics and Telecommunications Engineering 2018
Y. Chisik et al. (Eds.): INTETAIN 2017, LNICST 215, pp. 1–15, 2018.
https://doi.org/10.1007/978-3-319-73062-2_1

current attention is due to a novelty factor. Furthermore we want to understand whether the participants expect such games to be less predictable and to which extent they are regarded as animal abuse. For sake of brevity, in the remainder of this text we refer to living non-human organisms simply as organisms, and we refer to digital interactive (computer) games simply as games. But first we identify several categories of games that involve animals or other organisms.

2   Animal Incorporated Computer Games

If animals play, how animals play and why animals play are questions on which a lot of research has been conducted [7, 8]. It is not our intent to contribute to these questions in this article, since our goal is to study in which way the addition of an organism within a computer game changes the player's opinion on the game. There is quite a diversity of games which incorporate organisms. We choose to divide them by the type of inter-action the organism has within the game: voluntary interaction, involuntary interaction and indirect control.

2.1   Voluntary

With voluntary interaction we mean that the organism initiates the interaction or play on its own intent. Within the emerging field of ACI (Animal-Computer Interaction) [9] this freedom to engage or withdraw is a key aspect. Various games have been developed which allow pets and their owner to interact together [10–12]. Games can also be used to fight animal stress responses and resulting stereotypical behavior. Digital interactive gaming was shown to lower both behavioral and physiological (cortisol hormone) symptoms of stress in home-alone dogs [4]. A well-known game providing cognitive enrichment and physical exercise is *Pig Chase* [13], a game shared between humans and captive pigs via the internet that was proposed in 2012, but of which the current production status is undocumented. Moreover games to enrich the lives of captive orangutans are being researched [14].

There are also examples of games which could be played without human inter-ference. *Games for Cats* [2] is meant to be solely played by cats, but the game still requires human assistance since it involves navigating through menus and the free versions includes numerous popups. Similar games exist for dogs [15], but it remains uncertain if such games are beneficial for the dog's wellbeing [16]. Animals can also interact with regular games, as illustrated by a video in which a bullfrog tries to catch and eat ants from the popular mobile game *Ant Smasher* [17].

2.2   Involuntary

With involuntary interaction we mean that the animal does not initiate the interaction or play on its own intent. With such games the organism is incorporated within the game and responds to actions of the human player. Often these are natural mechanisms of survival, where the organism steers away from unfavorable conditions or is lured by favorable conditions. An example of a game employing involuntary interaction is a game by van Eck and Lamers [5], which is based around a modified Pac-Man game in which the opponent ghosts were controlled by living crickets inside a physical facsimile of the game level (maze). Vibrations within the physical maze stimulate the crickets to either chase the player's Pac-Man avatar or to avoid him, since for crickets vibrations indicate approaching danger from which they flee. Further examples are games for purposes of biology education [1, 18] and that embody an artistic endeavor [3]. Also the aforementioned *Ant Smasher* [17] game might be placed in this category, since it might be more likely the Bullfrog's intention is to eat, not to play.

2.3 Indirect

Indirect control of a game by organisms is also a possibility and illustrated by the project *Fish plays Pokémon* [19], in which a fish navigates a game of *Pokémon* (published by Nintendo, 1996) by swimming around its fish tank. Designated areas in the tank trigger actions within the game when entered by the fish. Variations on this principle were made with the games *Tetris* (various publishers) and *Street Fighter 2* (published by Capcom, 1991). In *Lumberjacked* [20] movements of the leaves of a tree are translated into movement of virtual tree characters. Organisms can furthermore be employed for content creation within a game. For example, in-game landscapes have been evolved in real-time based on the simultaneous growth of actual fungi and bacteria cultures in Petri dishes [6].

In the remainder of this work, we focus on an involuntary animal incorporated game [5] to study the expectations that humans have of playing such games. We realize that an involuntary type game by definition does not fulfill the requirements of the very relevant field of ACI. Still, since the main focus of this research lies on player expectations, we opted for a game which received notable media attention in, among others, popular gaming magazines, and of which gameplay footage is available. As mentioned in the introduction, our aim is to study why such a game received so much attention and the influence of the animal component on the reception of the game. Further motivations for our choice are argued in Sect. 5.

Although we have talked about the broad class of organisms until here, our study pertains to species of the phylogenetic branch of animals or Metazoa, thus excluding among others bacteria, fungi, slime molds, and plants. After discussing related other studies, we define our survey and analyze its results. With a concluding discussion we aim to give insight on human expectations of playing animal incorporated games, and its future directions.

3 Prior Studies of Players' (Expected) Experience

The difference in user experience between playing against a computer or against an opponent controlled by an organism was not yet empirically studied. Lee *et al.* [18] conducted a user experience study regarding a museum installation in which museum visitors interact with living cells. It displays a microscopic view of living cells through a touchscreen interface on which users can draw. These drawings are then projected onto the microscopy field as light patterns, causing phototactic responses and in turn motion of the cells. Various games and experiments are available to installation users requiring them to guide cells to a specific area on the screen or trap them within a virtual box. The study mainly concludes that museum visitors enjoyed interacting with the installation. Participants made positive comments about the inclusion of living cells and other aspects of the installation were praised. Since there was no comparison with a similar installation lacking a living organism we cannot identify the impact of the organisms' presence on user experience.

User reviews of commercially available animal incorporated type games could also offer insight on player experiences. In the Google Play Store and Apple's App Store numerous games are on offer which were developed to be played by cats. The abovementioned *Games for Cats* [2] allegedly has over 2 million downloads (November 2016) and numerous consumer reviews. Here we mostly read whether cats did or did not seem to like the games, roughly how long they were interested, whether the (presumed) pet owners enjoyed watching cats play, and comments on the app itself, e.g. about price and stability. Although user reviews provide potentially valuable information to assess user experiences, in this case they give us no clear comparison between games with and without opponents controlled by organisms.

Aforementioned Pac-Man study [5] that compares playing against an algorithmically controlled versus against an animal-controlled opponent created a context that enabled study of player experiences with the modified (animal incorporated) and standard (player-versus-computer) Pac-Man games, although it did not undertake such an empirical comparison.

Although not about games that incorporate organisms, a relevant study was undertaken by Weibel *et al.* [21]. It concluded that players who falsely believed they played an online game against human-controlled opponents experienced more enjoyment, presence and flow in doing so, when compared to players that were aware of the opponents' true algorithmic control. Generalizing this result from human-controlled opponents to organism-controlled opponents, one can hypothesize that similar positive change in player experience could occur—in other words, the mere idea of playing a game incorporated with living organisms may affect player experience. As a corollary, even without actual playing, the mere idea of organism-controlled opponents in a game may positively affect expected player experience.

Table 1 offers us a conceptual framework to categorize studies that investigate either player expectations or experiences given various assumed and actual opponents. With computer opponents, we mean algorithmically controlled opponents. Exact organism simulations are hypothetical algorithmically controlled opponents that exhibit perfect simulation of organism behavior. Studies wherein the actual opponent is none do not engage participants in actual game playing, but choose an alternative approach for data gathering such as surveys.

Within the conceptual classification framework, Weibel *et al.* [21] compare experiences from categories A and C. Although not empirically founded, van Eck and Lamers [5] compare categories A and F. In fact, the study described here compares player expectations for categories G, H and I, based on several hypotheses that are presented next.

Table 1. Conceptual classification framework for studying player expectations and experiences given various assumed and actual opponents. (*) Despite our earlier choice to reserve the term organism for non-human species, this does not apply within the context of the conceptual classification framework: here organism refers to living organisms of any species, including humans.

Actual opponent	Assumed opponent		
	Computer	Exact organism simulation (*)	Actual organism (*)
Computer	A	B	C
Actual organism (*)	D	E	F
None	G	H	I

4 Hypothesizing Players' Expectations

Our study of player expectations is formed around several hypotheses regarding player expectations about organism incorporated games. Here we state these hypotheses and their backgrounds. Some of the hypotheses are formulated as a comparative statement. For the sake of brevity, unless explicitly mentioned, we have left out the base condition to which the comparison pertains, namely that the game is alternatively played against an algorithmically controlled opponent, a.k.a. non-player character or artificial intelligence (AI). Moreover, we refer to "animals" in the plural form whereby we mean one or more animals, and all mentions of "players" (plural and single) refer to humans.

Hypothesis 1. An animal incorporated game is expected to be less predictable.
It is a challenge for game developers to achieve the same unpredictability in AI opponents as exhibited by human opponents [22]. Although animals may not come up with well-considered game tactics, their natural behavior may add unpredictability to an opponent. This was observed in the Pac-Man versus crickets study [5]: after several minutes of play it became common for the crickets to ignore the vibrations and remain still, thus effectively pausing the game, while one play session even had a cricket introduce a new game character (ghost) by shedding its skin.

Hypothesis 2. An animal incorporated game is expected to be more fun.
Pet owners traditionally engage with their pets in non-computer games for reasons of enjoyment. Transferring this aspect of traditional interspecies play into the realm of digital gaming, one can imagine people expecting this aspect to enhance enjoyment in animal incorporated games. Furthermore, interaction with animals which might be detested in real-life (e.g. cockroaches, spiders) might trigger strong emotional responses such as excitement and abhorrence.

Moreover, although animal incorporated games are gaining momentum, for many (including gamers), it is yet an unknown possibility. As such, novelty bias could influence their expected enjoyment. Lack of experience with animal incorporated games could potentially cause misconceptions about the actual experience of interacting with animals, leading to heightened expectations. Furthermore, as explained above through reference to a study by Weibel *et al.* [21], falsely perceived existence of a human opponent enhances experienced enjoyment for players. This result could potentially transfer to both non-human opponents and expected enjoyment.

Hypothesis 3. An animal incorporated game is expected to be more interesting than a game incorporating a hypothetical exact computer simulations of such animal.

It is potentially interesting to separate the impact of people's awareness about a non-human opponent from its factual implications for gameplay. If the same behavior of animal control could be achieved through a hypothetical exact computer simulation of such animal, would people expect animal incorporated games to be more interesting nonetheless? The foundations of this hypothesis are similar to those of hypothesis 2, but it attempts to compare against behaviorally identical "traditional" opponents.

Hypothesis 4. Animal incorporated games can be considered a form of animal abuse.

Animal welfare is a major aspect of animal-computer interaction research. Firstly, such research should itself respect the well-being of animals while experimenting to build new knowledge. Secondly, it should aim not only to avoid animal cruelty but also to improve the current conditions of various animals in all situations. Just as digital technology is used in many ways to improve our own lives (a role that computer gaming embraces), so should it be employed to the benefit of our pets, livestock, wildlife, etc. [9, 23].

Although improving animal welfare is not necessarily the main objective of animal incorporated games, it is worthwhile to consider people's expectations about its role in propagating animal cruelty. Regarding animal incorporated games in which biotechnology methods are used, so-called biotic games, an in-depth ethical analysis was presented by Harvey *et al.* [24].

5 Survey

Since our aim is to study the expected experience of animal incorporated type games, there is no need for participants to actually play such a game. Instead, a survey was undertaken among a population of people who were not (in particular) expected to have experienced actually playing animal incorporated type games. Several reasons exist to opt for this approach. Firstly, studying the actual experience of playing such games may be obfuscated by prior expectations. It is our goal to identify these prior expectations, in order to create a proper context for later study of actual play experiences. Secondly, actual playing could potentially make it difficult to offer a similar experience to all participants, since animal incorporated type games were observed to be less predictable [5] and might offer quite various experiences.

Instead of presenting our respondents with a general overview of animal incorporated type of games, we chose the abovementioned study of cricket-controlled Pac-Man ghosts [5] as a case example for our survey. This offers respondents a clear example of the topic instead of a potentially overwhelming summary. Moreover, since Pac-Man is an iconic game we expect respondents to have a basic understanding of the game's rules and how the algorithmically controlled ghosts in the standard game behave (for example that they have roughly constant speed). This enables respondents to compare the animal incorporated and standard versions of the game.

Alternative animal incorporated games such as *Playing with Pigs* [13] and *Cat Cat Revolution* [10] present new game concepts designed especially for animal incorporated gaming. As such they would (a) lack an implementation with computationally controlled opponents for comparison, (b) require explanation of the game rules, and (c) potentially direct respondents' focus towards the novel game concepts instead on the possible presence of animal opponents. A fictional animal incorporated type game could be used as the presented case example, but its lack of actual gameplay footage would make it more difficult for the respondents to imagine concrete gameplay.

Before being presented with survey questions, participants were shown a short introduction video that uses footage from the abovementioned study of cricket-controlled Pac-Man ghosts as an example game (98 s. total duration, of which 44 s. explanation about the game through on-screen text and images and 54 s. of gameplay footage accompanied by on-screen text).

After viewing the video, participants were asked to answer 16 questions. The first two questions verify whether the participants know the standard Pac-Man game and question how much they like it, while the third question asks if they ever heard of games in which humans interact with a living animal. Next we ask if they would prefer the standard Pac-Man game or the version in which one plays against an animal controlled opponent. Then we ask whether they think the animal controlled Pac-Man game will be less predictable than the standard game, whether they would prefer this added unpredictability, and whether using crickets to control the in game adversaries is considered animal abuse. We conclude the game related questions by asking whether they would prefer to play against either real crickets or an exact simulation of real cricket behavior, and again check which of the three variations (regular, animal controlled, simulation) they would prefer. Basic demographic information (age, gender, nationality, education, gaming experience) was queried and an opportunity for providing comments to the survey was given. The language of the survey and introductory video was English. The original survey and video materials can be viewed online[1].

5.1 Respondents

We collected results from 177 respondents. The majority of these ($n = 146$, 82%) were collected from bachelor students at The Hague University of Applied Sciences during various lectures within the Faculty of IT & Design. The authors of this work were not involved in these lectures. Another 26 (15%) were collected from bachelor and master students of various faculties at Leiden University during a public lecture organized by a student council, and given by one of the authors of this work. It should be noted that the lecture topics were unrelated to animal incorporated games and gaming in general. During break times or after lecture completion, attending students were shown the introductory video after which they were asked to answer the survey questions. The remaining 5 responses (3%) were collected via a public Google Forms site distributed via gaming forums.

---

[1] http://goo.gl/forms/5Zy5nachA5.

Of the collected results none were discarded, leaving us 177 data for analysis. A brief summary of respondent characteristics is presented in Table 2. Although we queried the respondents' level of education and nationality we choose to leave these out of the results. We afterwards realized that the surveys usage of the American educational system is probably confusing for the mostly European group of respondents, possibly resulting in incorrect answers. We discarded the results on nationality since part of the respondents selected multiple answers, probably their original nationality and current residency.

Table 2. Brief summary of respondent characteristics based on self-report.

Topic	Options	n	Fraction
Age	12–17	2	1%
	18–24	147	83%
	25–34	24	14%
	35–44	3	2%
	Unreported	1	1%
Gender	Female	60	34%
	Male	114	64%
	Unreported	3	2%
Gamer	Yes	102	58%
	No	74	42%
	Unreported	1	1%
Play games	Never	14	8%
	Once a year	13	7%
	Once a month	24	14%
	Once a week	24	14%
	Some days per week	63	36%
	Every day	36	20%
	Unreported	3	2%

5.2 Results

Almost all respondents ($n = 175, 99\%$) were familiar with the standard Pac-Man game and the majority either liked it "very much" ($n = 28, 16\%$), "a bit" ($n = 115, 65\%$) or "not so much" ($n = 28, 16\%$). Eighty-five percent ($n = 151$) of the respondents had not yet heard of computer games which you play against animals. Table 3 presents the main questions and results of this survey.

Twenty-three participants left a comment. Comments ranged from compliments (e.g. "Very interesting field of research!", "Fun experiment!", "Brilliant concept"), encouragements (e.g. "Good luck!", "Keep it up!"), suggestions (e.g. "Mice would be fun too", "I'd use something else than bugs. And make it very clear the animals are not being harmed") and personal statements (e.g. "I don't like insects to be fair").

Table 3. Main questions of the survey and their results ($n = 177$).

	n	Fraction
A. *Would you prefer to play the standard Pac-Man game or Pac-Man against an animal controlled opponent?*		
Standard Pac-Man	60	34%
Pac-Man versus an animal controlled opponent	76	43%
I don't know	41	23%
Unreported	0	0%
B. *Do you expect playing Pac-Man against an animal controlled opponent will be more fun on the long term?*		
I expect standard Pac-Man would always be more fun to play	23	13%
It would be more fun for a couple of times	86	49%
It would be more fun for a week	13	7%
It would be more fun for a month	7	4%
It would be more fun for a year	1	1%
I expect an animal controlled opponent is always more fun	20	11%
I don't know	26	15%
Unreported	1	1%
C. *Do you think the animal controlled Pac-Man game will be less predictable?*		
Yes	133	75%
No	29	16%
I don't know	15	8%
Unreported	0	0%
D. *If yes, would you prefer this added unpredictability?*		
Yes	110	62%
No	23	13%
I don't know	20	11%
Unreported	24	14%
E. *If it was possible to exactly simulate the behavior of the crickets, would you prefer this above playing against real crickets?*		
Yes	65	37%
No	59	33%
I don't know	52	29%
Unreported	1	1%
F. *Which Pac-Man variant would you prefer?*		
Standard Pac-Man game	55	31%
Pac-Man versus real crickets	51	29%
Pac-Man versus computer simulated behavior of crickets	51	29%
I don't know	20	11%
Unreported	0	0%
G. *Do you consider playing Pac-Man against crickets animal abuse?*		
Strongly agree	10	6%
Agree	20	11%

(*continued*)

Table 3. (*continued*)

	n	Fraction
Neutral	66	37%
Disagree	49	28%
Strongly disagree	30	17%
Unreported	2	1%

6 Discussion

We studied the expected experience of animal incorporated games, through the use of a survey. Respondents were asked to consider expected differences between games with animal-controlled opponents, algorithmically controlled opponents, and opponents who are exact computer simulations of animal behavior. Focus was placed on aspects of expected predictability of behavior, expected fun when playing, and potential animal abuse. The results can be used to create a proper context for later study of player experiences regarding this type of games, and in particular to assess aspects such as novelty bias regarding animal incorporated games.

Results indicate that respondents firmly expect that animal-controlled opponents add unpredictability to the gameplay (Table 3C). Moreover, the added unpredictability appears appealing, given that 62% of respondents indicated to prefer it (Table 3D). This confirms the first stated hypothesis that an animal incorporated game is expected to be less predictable.

When asked about expected enjoyment or fun (Table 3B), respondents appear somewhat dichotomous in their expectations. Expected duration of enjoyment shows a general skewed bell-shaped distribution, with a maximum at the qualitative notion of "a couple of times" (49%). Extending from this point in both directions along the spectrum of duration (towards "never" ("prefer standard game") in one direction (13%), and towards "for a year" (1%) in the other), the distribution decreases monotonously. However, beyond the qualitative duration "for a year", at the indeterminate notion of "always more fun" there is a sharp increase (11%). This appears to indicate that the expected duration of added enjoyment for the majority group of respondents ($n = 130$, 73%) is distributed roughly bell-shaped, yet that a smaller mutually exclusive group of respondents (11%) expects animal-controlled opponents to always offer more enjoyment than computationally controlled opponents. The remaining respondents indicated not to have an expectation of enjoyment duration (15%), or did not answer the question (1%).

In light of hypothesis 2 which states that an animal incorporated game is expected to be more fun, we conclude that in general respondents expect animal incorporated games to be "more fun" than playing against common algorithmically controlled opponents. However, overall the added enjoyment is expected to be of limited duration (Table 3B), with the exception of a smaller group of respondents expecting sustained added enjoyment. These results can be interpreted as an indication that for the majority of respondents (73%) the expected added fun is caused by a "novelty effect", whereas a much smaller group (11%) expect more sustained factors to cause added enjoyment.

Although such sustained factors were not all specifically hypothesized, candidate factors are expected unpredictability of animal behavior, psychological effects caused by awareness of animal opponents, and expected engagement within play by animals.

Regarding the hypothetical possibility of implementing exact simulations of animal behavior as a substitute for using real animals, preferences expressed in Table 3E were roughly uniformly distributed over the three offered alternatives: preference for real animals (37%), preference for exact simulation (33%), explicitly stating not to know the preference (29%). Interestingly, both the roughly equal fractions of stated preferences, and the relatively large fraction of respondents unknowing of their preference point towards an overall equal split between the two alternative approaches.

With regards to hypothesis 3 which states that game played against animals is expected to be more interesting than when played against exact computer simulations of animals, it is interesting to consider what expectations could lead to the three alternative answers in Table 3E. Firstly, one could assume that both a preference for exact behavioral simulation (Table 3E, "yes") and an unknown preference towards either of the stated approaches (Table 3E, "don't know") indicate that respondents expect animal incorporated games to impact only behavior of opponents, and not provide other benefits, such as added player enjoyment caused by awareness of animal opponents. Alternatively, a preference for animal opponents (Table 3E, "no") could indicate the opposite: that besides potential behavioral effects, animal incorporated games offer other benefits. Secondly, preference for exact behavioral simulation (Table 3E, "yes") could point at having negative connotations towards the use of animals in gaming.

The survey questions shown in Table 3F and E overlap in content. Table 4 illustrates how these two questions are co-answered by respondents. As expected, the following co-answers occur frequently: Table 3E "yes" and Table 3F "simulation", Table 3E "no" and Table 3F "crickets", Table 3E "don't know" and Table 3F "don't know". This illustrated consistency in cross-question answering.

Table 4. Co-answering matrix for survey questions regarding preference for either simulation or animal opponents.

Prefer simulation above crickets? (Table 3E)	Which Pac-Man variant would you prefer? (Table 3F)				
	Standard	Simulation	Crickets	I don't know	Unreported
Yes	15	36	10	4	0
I don't know	19	8	12	13	0
No	21	6	29	3	0
Unreported	0	1	0	0	0

Pearson's Chi-square test was applied on the data of Table 4, excluding the "unreported" row and column. Results ($n = 176$, $p < 0.0001$) indicate that co-occurring answers deviate with statistical significance from their expected values under a null-hypothesis of no correlation. This outcome supports the a-priori expectation that the abovementioned answers strongly co-occur.

With respect to hypothesis 4, which states that an animal incorporated game can be considered a form of animal abuse, clearly opinions are divided, but not polarized (Table 3G). As mentioned earlier in regards to hypothesis 3, a preference for exact behavioral simulation over animal opponents could point at having negative connotations towards the use of animals in gaming. Table 5 illustrates the co-occurrence of such preferences (Table 3E) with answers regarding animal abuse (Table 3G). If leaving the "unreported" answers outside consideration, one could a-priori expect a co-occurrence pattern that appears stronger in the top-left, middle section and bottom-right of the co-answering matrix. Generally, this pattern is confirmed, with the exception of co-answers within the column "strongly agree". Oddly, respondents who agree strongly with the abuse-statement (Table 3G), would overall prefer playing against animals over simulated opponents when given this choice. An explanation for this seemingly contradictory aspect of otherwise logical answer co-occurrences in Table 5 is provided by the following statistical analysis.

Table 5. Co-answering matrix for survey questions Table 3E and G.

Prefer simulation above crickets? (Table 3E)	Do you consider playing Pac-Man against crickets animal abuse? (Table 3G)					
	Strongly agree	Agree	Neutral	Disagree	Strongly disagree	Unreported
Yes	1	12	30	15	6	1
I don't know	3	3	15	19	11	1
No	6	5	21	14	13	0
Unreported	0	0	0	1	0	0

Pearson's Chi-square test applied to Table 5, excluding the "unreported" row and column, indicates that co-occurring answers deviate with minor statistical significance from a pattern of no correlation ($n = 174$, $p < 0.05$). However, a common underlying assumption of the test, namely that all expected values under the null-hypothesis exceed 4, is not met for the top three cells in column "strongly agree", but is met for all other expected co-occurrences. This indicates that the odd results for said column are caused by underrepresentation in the sample data, whereas the a-priori expected distribution of co-occurring answers is met with statistical significance. Statistical significance ($n = 164$, $p < 0.05$) and the underlying assumptions are upheld when applying the same test excluding also column "strongly agree". This affirms our observation that preference for a simulated over real animal opponent is correlated and potentially modulated by considerations of animal welfare.

A similar co-answering matrix is presented in Table 6, correlating answers regarding animal abuse with preference between algorithmic opponent and animal opponent. Leaving the "unreported" answers outside consideration, here too we find the expected pattern of strong co-occurrence in top-left, middle section and bottom-right of the co-answering matrix. As in Table 5, expected values under the Chi-square test's null hypothesis of no correlation are too low in column "strongly agree", violating one of the test's underlying assumptions. Excluding said column, the sample data meet all underlying assumptions of the test. Applying Pearson's Chi-square test as above, both including and excluding column "strongly agree", yields results that are statistically significant (resp. $n = 175$, $p < 0.005$, and $n = 165$, $p < 0.05$). As in Table 5 also, these data and statistical test results indicate that preference for potential animal opponents is significantly correlated and potentially modulated by considerations of animal welfare.

Table 6. Co-answering matrix for survey questions Table 3A and G.

Standard Pac-Man or versus crickets? (Table 3A)	Do you consider playing Pac-Man against crickets animal abuse? (Table 3G)					
	Strongly agree	Agree	Neutral	Disagree	Strongly disagree	Unreported
Standard Pac-Man	8	13	19	14	6	0
I don't know	1	2	18	13	5	2
Versus crickets	1	5	29	22	19	0
Unreported	0	0	0	0	0	0

Having discussed the results in relation to the four hypotheses stated, it is time to reflect on the meaning of it all. Animal incorporated type of games are strongly expected to add unpredictability to opponent behavior, and respondents expect that this unpredictability is a preferable. Furthermore, they are generally expected to be "more fun" than playing against algorithmically controlled opponents, although the added enjoyment is expected to be of limited duration. This hints at a novelty effect in expected player enjoyment. Naturally, this result does not consider animal enjoyment, or other aspects of animal well-being. Although considerations of animal abuse are difficult to quantify exactly from the data, it is clearly a present factor of concern. Moreover, we do find multiple quantitative and statistically significant indications that willingness to play animal incorporated games, instead of common computer opponents or hypothetical exact simulations of animals, is moderated by animal welfare concerns.

Naturally, our study does not cover all the possible aspects to consider in understanding player preferences for animal incorporated type of games. It is an initial venture into the study of acceptance of such games. To complete the picture, alternative aspects such as animal volition to play, regards of animal species, animal roles (wildlife, livestock, pets) and many more, should be studied.

With regards to methodological implications we recognize and accept the limitations. A potentially striking choice is the selection of a specific example case (crickets and Pac-Man) upon which to base the survey introduction and questions. Naturally, the approach chosen could influence the results, and we have explained our reasoning for this choice extensively in Sect. 4. Nonetheless, the fact that the crickets did not partake voluntarily and were stimulated with vibrations could affect respondents' emotions and answers[2], potentially affecting results regarding three of the four stated hypotheses. More general methodological implications include the gathering of data through self-report, and the possibility that respondents did not correctly understand the meaning of hypothetical "exact simulation" of animal behavior.

Results should be considered with respect to their correct scoping. In particular, expectations are not experiences. We have indicated at the onset of this work that it deals with player expectation, which may be different from actual (future) experiences. Naturally, a sample of generally Dutch students is not representative for the diversity of culture, age, experience, personal situation, etcetera of a general population. Logistic constraints have contributed to these scoping boundaries.

To better understand the player's experience, our next step will be to conduct a study on the *actual* player experience using an animal incorporated type game developed solely for this purpose. The findings of this article will support us in making more informed decisions regarding both our game design and our experiment design.

We are confident to have presented a valuable initial venture into studying the acceptance of animal incorporated type of games. As this work deals with expectations, we expect that this challenging topic will be further unraveled by us and others.

References

1. Riedel-Kruse, I.H., Chung, A.M., Dura, B., Hamilton, A.L., Lee, B.C.: Design, engineering and utility of biotic games. Lab Chip **11**(1), 14–22 (2011). https://doi.org/10.1039/C0LC00399A
2. Purina Friskies: Games for Cats (2011). https://www.gamesforcats.com
3. Wilson, S.: Protozoa Games (2003). http://userwww.sfsu.edu/swilson/art/protozoagames/protogames10.html
4. Geurtsen, A., Lamers, M.H., Schaaf, M.J.M.: Interactive digital gameplay can lower stress hormone levels in home alone dogs—a case for animal welfare informatics. In: Chorianopoulos, K., Divitini, M., Hauge, J.B., Jaccheri, L., Malaka, R. (eds.) ICEC 2015. LNCS, vol. 9353, pp. 238–251. Springer, Cham (2015). https://doi.org/10.1007/978-3-319-24589-8_18
5. van Eck, W., Lamers, M.H.: Animal controlled computer games: playing Pac-Man against real crickets. In: Harper, R., Rauterberg, M., Combetto, M. (eds.) ICEC 2006. LNCS, vol. 4161, pp. 31–36. Springer, Heidelberg (2006). https://doi.org/10.1007/11872320_4
6. van Eck, W., Lamers, M.H.: Biological content generation: evolving game terrains through living organisms. In: Johnson, C., Carballal, A., Correia, J. (eds.) EvoMUSART 2015. LNCS, vol. 9027, pp. 224–235. Springer, Cham (2015). https://doi.org/10.1007/978-3-319-16498-4_20
7. Fagen, R.: Animal Play Behaviour. Oxford University Press, New York (1981)
8. Smith, P.K.: Play in Animals and Humans. Blackwell Pub, Oxford (1986)
9. Mancini, C.: Animal-computer interaction: a manifesto. Interactions **18**(4), 69–73 (2011). https://doi.org/10.1145/1978822.1978836

---

[2] As one respondent indicated on the survey, "*I do not like crickets!*".

10. Noz, F., An, J.: Cat cat revolution: an interspecies gaming experience. In: Proceedings of SIGCHI Conference on Human Factors in Computing Systems, pp. 2661–2664 (2011). https://doi.org/10.1145/1978942.1979331

11. Tan, R.T.K.C., Cheok, A.D., Peiris, R., Todorovic, V., Loi, H.C., Loh, C.W., Derek, T.B.S.: Metazoa ludens: mixed reality interactions and play for small pets and humans. Leonardo **41** (3), 308–309 (2008). https://doi.org/10.1162/leon.2008.41.3.308

12. Westerlaken, M., Stefano G.: Felino: the philosophical practice of making an interspecies videogame. In: The Philosophy of Computer Games Conference, pp. 1–12 (2014)

13. Alfrink, K., van Peer, I., Lagerweij, H., Driessen, C., Bracke, M.: Playing with Pigs (2012). http://www.playingwithpigs.nl

14. Wirman, H.: Games for/with strangers-captive orangutan (pongo pygmaeus) touch screen play. Antennae **30**, 105–115 (2014)

15. Extra Pop.: Games for dogs (2015). http://www.bicshare.com

16. Baskin, S., Zamansky, A., Kononova, V.: Exploring human perceptions of dog tablet playful interactions. In: Proceedings of Third International Conference on Animal-Computer Interaction (2016). https://doi.org/10.1145/2995257.3012023

17. Youtube: African Bull Frog ant crusher (2011). youtu.be/WlEzvdlYRes

18. Lee, S.A., Bumbacher, E., Chung, A.M., Cira, N., Walker, B., Park, J.Y., Starr, B., Blikstein, P., Riedel-Kruse, I.H.: Trap it!: a playful human-biology interaction for a museum installation. In: Proceedings of 33rd Annual ACM Conference on Human Factors in Computing Systems (2015). https://doi.org/10.1145/2702123.2702220

19. Youtube: Fish plays Pokemon: pallet town syndrome (2014). youtu.be/48-qOC4fCdk

20. Young, D.: Lumberjacked (2005). http://classic.rhizome.org/artbase/artwork/35526

21. Weibel, D., Wissmath, B., Habegger, S., Steiner, Y., Groner, R.: Playing online games against computer- vs. human-controlled opponents: effects on presence, flow, and enjoyment. Comput. Hum. Behav. **24**(5), 2274–2291 (2008). https://doi.org/10.1016/j.chb.2007.11.002

22. Rouse, R.: Game Design: Theory and Practice, 2nd edn. Jones and Barlett Publishers, Sudbury (2005)

23. Mancini, C., Zamansky, A.: Charting unconquered territories: intelligent systems for animal welfare. In: 40th Annual Convention of the Society for the Study of Artificial Intelligence and the Simulation of Behaviour, pp. 181–182 (2014)

24. Harvey, H., Havard, M., Magnus, D., Cho, M.K., Riedel-Kruse, I.H.: Innocent fun or 'microslavery'. Hastings Cent. Rep. **44**(6), 38–46 (2014). https://doi.org/10.1002/hast.386

Reaper Tournament System

Nhien Pham Hoang Bao, Shuo Xiong[(✉)], and Hiroyuki Iida

Japan Advanced Institute of Science and Technology,
1-1 Asahidai, Nomi 923-1292, Japan
{phbnhien,xiongshuo,iida}@jaist.ac.jp

Abstract. This paper explores a novel way for analyzing tournament structures. Our goal is to find the best suitable tournament under considered purposes. Aside from the number of matches, we address on two other important aspects: competitiveness development and ranking precision. Competitiveness development emphasizes the importance participants' motivation in every match while keeping the matches exciting throughout the tournament. Ranking precision reflects the credibility of tournament results, so that prizes can be distributed with minimum complains and dissatisfaction. To address competitiveness development, this paper proposes a new method which visualizes tournament structures as a tree using graphical model approach, which we call *progress tree*. Considering the similarities of sorting algorithm with the ranking process, ranking precision is discussed based on the quality of algorithm for the ranking task. This paper also analyzes well known tournament structures such as single elimination, double elimination, round robin and Swiss system. The performed analysis reveals the strength and weakness of each tournament structure. Although each tournament has its own pros and cons, none of them can convince the tournament results for all participants while keeping the matches strongly motivating thoroughly. Thus, a new tournament structure called *reaper tournament system* is proposed in this paper to meet those requirements.

Keywords: Tournament structure · Competitiveness development
Stability progressing · Ranking precision

1 Introduction

Competitive games do not just attract players only, but also many spectators who are interested in the game. Tournament is a competitive system to identify the winners. It usually provides some prizes as objectives for participants to compete against each other. It is often used as a formal method to conduct an official game event, to gather players or teams, as well as to attract a large number of spectators. Such large scale events usually receive sponsorship from various companies and organizations. Therefore, it is necessary to be carefully prepared and conducted to be able to avoid disappointments from any party.

© ICST Institute for Computer Sciences, Social Informatics and Telecommunications Engineering 2018
Y. Chisik et al. (Eds.): INTETAIN 2017, LNICST 215, pp. 16–33, 2018.
https://doi.org/10.1007/978-3-319-73062-2_2

Let us discuss three main concerns in tournament systems.

1. The number of matches. This number is crucial for the tournament organizer to calculate the cost of conducting the tournament.
2. Competitiveness development (CD). That is, to avoid the throwaway matches in which participants are not so motivated to play their best. Regarding competitive games, uneven teams tend to make a reduce of interest from the viewers [13,14,18]. However, the structure of the tournament may have great effect on the motivation of the participants. It is important to plan the matches carefully, giving the participants good motivations to play their best in the game.
3. Ranking precision (RP). That is, to make sure the ranking results of a tournament are convincing and reliable. It is important to prove that the prize winners are really worthy.

Regarding the checking of a tournament for whether it can maintain the competitiveness, to the best of our knowledge, there has been until now no study of any method to perform this work. Therefore, we propose a new method to analyze the tournament structures.

The structure of the paper is as follows. Section 2 presents our method for analyzing tournament structures with a focus on competitiveness development and ranking precision. Section 3 shows an analysis of tournament structures including single-elimination, double-elimination, round-robin, and Swiss system. Section 3.6 discusses and analyzes results and evaluation. Section 4 proposes a new tournament system called *reaper tournament*, and analyzes it. Finally, concluding remarks are given in Sect. 5.

2 Analyzing Method

This section presents two important aspects of tournament systems: competitiveness development and ranking precision.

2.1 Competitiveness Development

A competitive match means that the two participants are motivated to compete over the winning outcome. Usually, the desire to win is normal. But, sometimes the benefit of winning could not be so significant, which causes the participants to not yearn for a win. The motivation of a participant consists of many factors, but we restrict ourselves to the tournament structure in this paper. We introduce a notion of "progress tree" to demonstrate the perspective of the participants in a tournament, and then analyze the development of their motivation throughout the tournament.

The progress tree is constructed based on the graphical model approach [17]. A participant's state before or after playing a match is considered as a node. The state in which the participant no longer plays any match is a leaf node. We

Fig. 1. Single elimination tournament for 8 participants

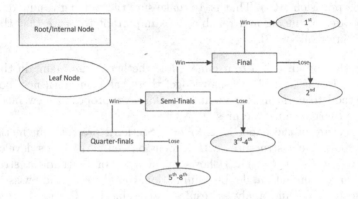

Fig. 2. Progress tree of single elimination tournament for 8 participants

show, in Fig. 1, an example of a single elimination tournament for 8 participants, and Fig. 2 shows its progress tree[1].

While "competitive" means having an objective for which participants have to compete against another one, it is common to have more than one prize as objectives in a tournament. Thus, it is necessary to provide prizes that are comparable in order to ensure the consistency in competitiveness. For example, if two winners receive a spoon as the first prize and a pair of chopsticks as the second prize. Each participant may evaluate these prizes differently. Hence, it is possible that a participant would try to lose on purpose in the final match to obtain the pair of chopsticks. This is also the reason why most grand tournaments use money for prizes instead of objects, since the amounts of money are comparable, the consistency between the prizes is ensured.

With consistent prizes in the same unit, we can evaluate nodes in the progress tree. Since we are only considering the structure of the tournament, we evaluate a node as the average value of its direct child nodes. For example, in Fig. 2, let x_1, x_2, x_3 and x_4 be the 1st place prize, 2nd prize, 3rd-4th prize and 5th-8th prize

---

[1] In this paper, we assume that a match can only result in a win or a loss.

respectively. Then we have $x_1 \geq x_2 \geq x_3 \geq x_4$. Table 1 shows the evaluation (called the *stability value*) for each node of the progress tree in Fig. 2.

Table 1. Stability values for each node of progress tree in Fig. 2

Node level	Stability value
Final (v)	$\frac{x_1 + x_2}{2}$
Semi-final (v_1)	$\frac{v + x_3}{2}$
Quarter-final (v_2)	$\frac{v_1 + x_4}{2}$

With the progress tree and having the nodes evaluated, we see that there are two concerns regarding player's motivation or competitiveness development.

Stability progressing. For every node, it is preferable to have the value of the winning outcome larger than the value of the losing outcome. This ensures that the winning outcome has more benefits and is more attractive for the participant.

Possibility of results. Since the prizes serve as an objective to maintain competitiveness, the case in which a prize is no longer able to be achieved also means that a competitive objective is lost. However, in a tournament, to achieve a prize means to give up other prizes (one cannot get the first prize and second prize together). Therefore, it is favorable to have the prizes dropping out eventually in the order of least-valuable first. This practice can also be seen in most prize announcements from lottery prizes to singing/beauty contests.

Aside from those above-mentioned points, there might be a few more interesting observations we can make with the progress tree. For example, if there is a match between two participants who are not on the same node, which means that they are not on an equal footing; the importance of the match, and their motivation of the match are different.

2.2 Ranking Precision

Being a competitive system, the outcome of a tournament should avoid any complaints about its ranking results. This task for giving rankings to the tournament participants is similar to the sorting by comparisons: the input is a list of members to be compared, while the output is a permutation of the input with the member in an order. Although actual sorting algorithms [1–3,7,8,10,15,19] may not be suitable to be applied as tournament systems because they do not consider fair treatment to participants with the same performance, it is crucial for a tournament system to maintain the convincement of the rankings to minimize complains from participants and spectators.

We assume that there is a game in which we compare credits, where the participant with higher credits wins. The ranking precision of the tournament is derived from how the tournament can rank participants correctly for such a game. In other words, we consider the tournament as a sorting algorithm, and each match is a comparison between two participants in a game whose outcome is deterministic. Providing all participants with different credits, we run all possible simulations by using permutation. Then, we can see whether or not the tournament can give rankings to participants correctly. However, the method of using permutation simulation is too heavy if the number of participants is too large. In this paper, we therefore conduct experiments with eight participants only.

3   Analysis of Standard Tournament Systems

We analyze several standard tournament systems such as single elimination, double elimination, round-robin and Swiss system. For the purpose of comparison, we consider the example of having eight participants in each case.

3.1   Single Elimination

Single elimination is a type of elimination tournament where the loser of each bracket is immediately eliminated.

Number of Matches: A standard single elimination system with i rounds has $n = 2^i$ participants, and there will be $m = n - 1$ matches conducted. For 8 players single elimination, there would be 7 matches with 3 rounds.

Competitiveness Development: We use the example of 8 participants single elimination, as previously shown in Fig. 1. Assuming that this tournament has comparable prizes distributed in the right order, by observing Fig. 2 and Table 1, we can see that it has no issues regarding *stability progressing* or *possibility of results*. All wins are worth aiming for, and the ranking results are decided from the lowest ranking first.

Ranking Precision: We run the simulations for 8 participants with credits varying from 1 to 8. Table 2 shows the precise ranking of the tournament, while Table 3 shows the actual results counting all (8! = 40320) permutations.

Remark 1. *Among all ranking results, the only 100% correct one is the 1st place. This suggests that single elimination provides the reliable ranking results for the first place only, and other rankings are not really convincing.*

Table 2. The precise ranking of single elimination

Participant	Precise ranking
8	1st place
7	2nd place
6	3–4th place
5	3–4th place
4	5–8th place
3	5–8th place
2	5–8th place
1	5–8th place

Table 3. The results of ranking simulation of single elimination

Participant	1st place	2nd place	3–4th place	5–8th place
1	0 (0%)	0 (0%)	0 (0%)	40320 (100%)
2	0 (0%)	0 (0%)	5760 (14%)	34560 (86%)
3	0 (0%)	0 (0%)	11520 (29%)	28800 (71%)
4	0 (0%)	1152 (3%)	16128 (40%)	23040 (57%)
5	0 (0%)	4608 (11%)	18432 (46%)	17280 (43%)
6	0 (0%)	11520 (29%)	17280 (43%)	11520 (29%)
7	0 (0%)	23040 (57%)	11520 (29%)	5760 (14%)
8	40320 (100%)	0 (0%)	0 (0%)	0 (0%)

3.2   Double Elimination (Classic)

A classic double elimination tournament is designed for at least four participants. At first participants are paired up one on one. The losers will be placed into the lower bracket, whereas the winners will be placed in upper brackets. From this point on, if a participant from the loser's bracket loses a game, the participant is eliminated; if a participant from the winner's bracket loses, the participant will be moved to the loser's bracket. The last participant remaining in the lower bracket will face the last participant standing in the upper bracket in the grand final. This means that after the bracket arranging round at the beginning and before the grand final, for every upper bracket's round, there would be two rounds in the lower bracket.

Number of Matches: A classic double-elimination tournament system for $n = 2^i$ participants (where $1 < i \in \mathbb{N}$) will have $m = 2n - 2$ matches conducted. Thus, we have $m = 14$ when $n = 8$.

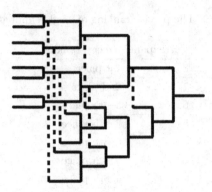

Fig. 3. Classic double elimination tournament for 8 participants

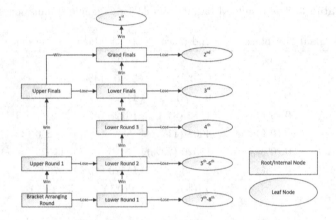

Fig. 4. Progress tree of classic double-elimination tournament

Competitiveness Development: We show, in Fig. 3, a classic double-elimination tournament for 8 participants, and Fig. 4 shows its progress tree.

Assuming that this tournament has comparable prizes distributed in the right order, by observing Fig. 6, we can see that it has no issues regarding *stability progressing* or *possibility of results*. Every win has a more favorable value than its loss, and the ranking results are decided from the lowest ranking first.

Ranking Precision: We run the simulations for 8 participants with credits varying from 1 to 8. Table 4 shows the precise ranking of the tournament, while Table 5 shows the actual results counting all $8! = 40320$ permutations.

Remark 2. *Our analysis suggests that the classic double-elimination tournament provides reliable ranking result for the first and second place. Still, the other rankings are not really convincing.*

Table 4. The precise ranking of double elimination

Participant	Precise ranking
8	1st place
7	2nd place
6	3rd place
5	4th place
4	5–6th place
3	5–6th place
2	7–8th place
1	7–8th place

Table 5. The results of ranking simulation of classic double elimination

P.	1st place	2nd place	3rd place	4th place	5–6th place	7–8th place
1	0 (0%)	0 (0%)	0 (0%)	0 (0%)	0 (0%)	40320 (100%)
2	0 (0%)	0 (0%)	0 (0%)	0 (0%)	17280 (43%)	23040 (57%)
3	0 (0%)	0 (0%)	0 (0%)	0 (0%)	28800 (71%)	11520 (29%)
4	0 (0%)	0 (0%)	1152 (3%)	9216 (23%)	25344 (63%)	4608 (11%)
5	0 (0%)	0 (0%)	4608 (11%)	25344 (63%)	9216 (23%)	1152 (3%)
6	0 (0%)	0 (0%)	34560 (86%)	5760 (14%)	0 (0%)	0 (0%)
7	0 (0%)	40320 (100%)	0 (0%)	0 (0%)	0 (0%)	0 (0%)
8	40320 (100%)	0 (0%)	0 (0%)	0 (0%)	0 (0%)	0 (0%)

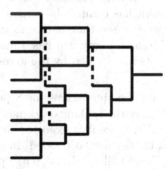

Fig. 5. Seeded double-elimination tournament for 8 participants

3.3   Double Elimination (Seeded)

In recent double-elimination tournament systems, the bracket arranging round is considered as a pre-stage. This pre-stage can take other forms of tournaments [4,5], or use a rating system [6,9,11,12,16,20] to divide (seed) participants into upper and lower brackets. The rest works the same as in the classic double-elimination tournament.

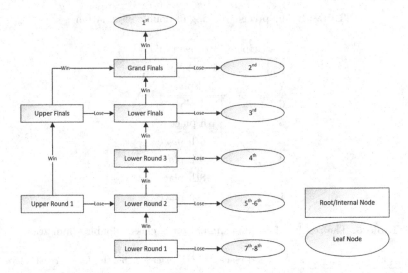

Fig. 6. Progress tree of seeded double-elimination tournament for 8 participants

Number of Matches: A standard seeded double-elimination tournament system with i upper rounds has $n = 2^i$ participants, and there will be $m = \frac{3}{2}n - 2$ matches conducted. Thus, we have $m = 10$ when $n = 8$.

Competitiveness Development: We show, in Fig. 5, a seeded double-elimination tournament for 8 participants, and Fig. 6 shows its progress tree. Assuming that this tournament has comparable prizes distributed in the right order, by observing Fig. 6, we can see that it has no issues regarding *stability progressing* or *possibility of results*. Every win has a more favorable value than its loss, and the ranking results are decided by the lowest ranking first.

Ranking Precision: We run the simulations for 8 participants with credits varying from 1 to 8. Table 4 shows the ranking outcome of the tournament, while Table 6 shows the actual results. Since it is expected that stronger participants and weaker participants will be distributed (seeded) into the upper bracket and the lower bracket properly, There will be $4! \times 4! = 576$ permutations.

Remark 3. *The results (Table 6) of the seeded double-elimination show that it is precise from the 1st to the 4th ranking. This is quite a big improvement compared to the systems we analyzed previously. However, this reliability is heavily based on the seeding system, which may cost many more matches.*

3.4   Round-Robin

In the round-robin tournament system, all participants have to play with each other. In other words, each participant plays with every other participant once. If each participant plays all others twice, the system is called *double round-robin*.

Table 6. Ranking results of seeded double elimination for 8 participants experiment

P.	1st place	2nd place	3rd place	4th place	5–6th place	7–8th place
1	0 (0%)	0 (0%)	0 (0%)	0 (0%)	0 (0%)	576 (100%)
2	0 (0%)	0 (0%)	0 (0%)	0 (0%)	192 (33%)	384 (67%)
3	0 (0%)	0 (0%)	0 (0%)	0 (0%)	384 (67%)	192 (33%)
4	0 (0%)	0 (0%)	0 (0%)	0 (0%)	576 (100%)	0 (0%)
5	0 (0%)	0 (0%)	0 (0%)	576 (100%)	0 (0%)	0 (0%)
6	0 (0%)	0 (0%)	576 (100%)	0 (0%)	0 (0%)	0 (0%)
7	0 (0%)	576 (100%)	0 (0%)	0 (0%)	0 (0%)	0 (0%)
8	576 (100%)	0 (0%)	0 (0%)	0 (0%)	0 (0%)	0 (0%)

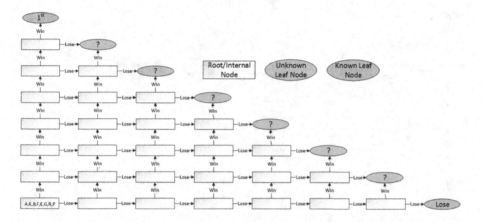

Fig. 7. The first round of progress tree of round-robin tournament for 8 participants

Number of Matches: A round-robin system for n participants consists of $m = \frac{n}{2}(n-1)$ matches conducted. Thus for 8 participants, there would be $m = 28$ matches.

Competitiveness Development: We show, in Fig. 7, a progress tree of a round-robin tournament with 8 participants. The big difference from elimination tournaments is that from the beginning, only the leaf from all losses and the leaf from all wins are known. This unstable situation makes us unable to calculate the stability values of the nodes. As the tournament progresses, the unknown leaves will gradually reveal themselves, and the stability values of the nodes would be calculated. Furthermore, unstable situations suggest that it is possible that *stability progressing* and *possibility of results* conditions are not satisfied.

We show, in Table 7, an example situation after 5 rounds, and Fig. 8 shows its progress tree. In this situation, if participant A wins the next match, his victory as the 1st place would be fixed regardless of his last match outcome. This fails to satisfy *stability progressing*. Besides, even the leaves of participants

Table 7. An example of round-robin tournament progress after 5 rounds

Participant	Wins	Losses
A	5	0
K	3	2
B	2	3
F	2	3
E	2	3
G	2	3
R	2	3
P	2	3

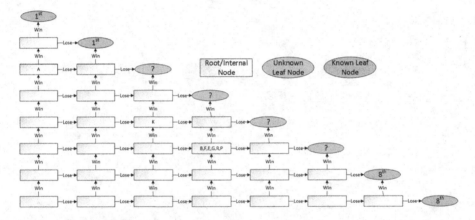

Fig. 8. Progress tree for the round-robin tournament progress presented in Table 7

B, F, E, G, R, and P are unknown, the possibility of 1st place is certainly out of reach. Therefore, this situation does not satisfy the *possibility of results* condition either.

Ranking Precision: We run the simulations for 8 participants with credits varying from 1 to 8. Then, there is only one outcome as shown in Table 8, no matter how the participants are positioned.

Remark 4. *Round-robin tournament gives a really accurate ranking in the simulation. However, the number of matches is high, and the competitiveness development is not good.*

3.5 Swiss System

The Swiss tournament system or the Swiss System is a round based, non-eliminating system that in every round each participant is matched against

Table 8. The result of round-robin tournament

Participant	Wins	Losses	Ranking
8	7	0	1st place
7	6	1	2nd place
6	5	2	3rd place
5	4	3	4th place
4	3	4	5th place
3	2	5	6th place
2	1	6	7th place
1	0	7	8th place

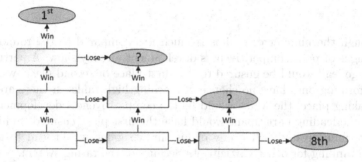

Fig. 9. Progress tree of the Swiss System for 8 participants with 3 rounds

another with a similar score, but not with the same opponent more than once. The number of rounds is considerably less than in a round-robin system. Every participant has to play every round, unless the number of participants is odd. After all the rounds have taken place, if there are participants with the same scores, they will be ranked based on a rating system chosen by the tournament organizer.

We conduct our analysis on an 8 players Swiss System. Assuming that there are no drawn games, and three rounds would be needed.

Number of Matches: A standard Swiss System would require the same number of rounds as a single elimination tournament to determine a clear winner. Thus, for n participants it has $m = \frac{n}{2}(\frac{n}{2} - 1)$ matches conducted. Thus, Swiss System for 8 participants with 3 rounds would consist of $m = 12$ matches.

Competitiveness Development: We show, in Fig. 9, the progress tree of the Swiss System for 8 participants with 3 rounds. The leaf nodes of this system are special. If more than one participant reaches the same leaf node, those participants would be ranked by a rating system chosen by the tournament organizer.

Table 9. The expected and actual ranking results of the Swiss System for 8 participants with 3 rounds

Participant	Expected ranking	Precision
1	8th place	40320 (100%)
2	7th place	23040 (57%)
3	6th place	16128 (40%)
4	5th place	15360 (38%)
5	4th place	13440 (33%)
6	3rd place	16128 (40%)
7	2nd place	25088 (62%)
8	1st place	40320 (100%)

Although the number of rounds is much less compared to the round-robin system, signs of poor competitiveness development already show. A participant with a large lead would be ensured to take first place or second place, while the poor performing ones have no chance of reaching high ranks. If there are more rounds taking place, the worse would be the competitiveness development. For example, the leading participant would have the first place ensured, so his final games are unmotivated; while any of his thrown game would lead to a large change in ranking for other participants because of the rating system.

Ranking Precision: We run the simulations for 8 participants with credits varying from 1 to 8. Table 9 shows the expected precise ranking of the tournament as well as the actual results counting all 8! = 40320 permutations of Swiss System with 3 rounds.

Remark 5. *The ranking precision of the Swiss System is only reliable for the first place and the last place, while the ranking for the other participants is not. Increasing the number of rounds might gradually lead to better results. However, as mentioned in the competitiveness development section, the last games of the top participant might be unmotivated, yet its effects on the ranking of the opponents and other middle ranking participants. This furthermore causes the middle rankings to be unstable.*

3.6   Summary

We show in Table 10 the comparison between the single elimination, double elimination, round-robin and Swiss tournament system. The results show that the single-elimination system has the lowest cost, while its competitiveness development is properly maintained. However, its ranking is only reliable for the top winner. Double-elimination has no problem in competitiveness development either. Its classic style can convincingly qualify the top two winners, while its seeded system can qualify the top four winners. Round-robin on the other hand gives

Table 10. Strength and weakness of the common tournaments compared by the number of matches with n players ($n = 8$), competitiveness development (CD) and ranking precision. Note that the number of matches for the double-elimination (seeded) might be higher when counting the pre-stages.

Tournament system	Matches (for n = 8)	CD	Ranking precision
Single elimination	$n - 1 = 7$	✓	Top 1 winner only
Double elimination (classic)	$2n - 2 = 14$	✓	Top 2 winners
Double elimination (seeded)	$\frac{3}{2}n - 2 = 10$	✓	Top 4 winners
Round robin	$\frac{n}{2}(n - 1) = 28$	✗	All
Swiss System	$\frac{n}{2}(\frac{n}{2} - 1) = 12$	✗	Top 1 winner & last place

convincing ranking on all participants, but it lacks in competitiveness development, and its number of matches is the largest. Swiss system has reliable ranking for the top winner and the last place, whilst the middle rankings are not. The Swiss system also has poor competitive development.

4 Reaper Tournament System

As the results above show, there is no tournament systems which can satisfy both the competitiveness development and the ranking precision for all participants requirement. Thus, we propose a new tournament system called *reaper tournament system*. It assumes the participant number $n = 2^i$ with $1 < i \in \mathbb{N}$.

4.1 The Regulation

Each participant has a list of respected opponents (called respect list) which includes all of the opponents the participant has previously lost to. The reaper tournament system consists of the following steps.

1. **Reaper selection:** All the participants are paired up one on one, the losers will continue to be paired again until there are only two left. These two who have the worst performance will play with each other and the loser will be eliminated as the last place, while the winner will be the reaper. Go to step 2.
2. **Reaper candidates:** The eliminated participants will have their respect list ignored. Aside from the reaper and the eliminated participant(s), all participants who are not in any respect list are placed in a candidate list. If every remaining participant is in a respect list, then the list of candidates will consist of participants which are only respected by the reaper. If there is more than 1 candidate, to step 3. If there is one candidate, to step 4. If there is none, the reaper tournament ends.
3. **Candidates match:** The top two best performance participants in the candidates list will play a match. Of course the winner will be added to the loser's respect list. Go back to step 2.

4. **Reaper match:** The participant in the candidates list will play against the reaper. The loser from the reaper match will be eliminated and will be ranked just above the previously eliminated participant, while the winner will be the (new) reaper, the system repeatedly finds the weakest player for elimination. Go to step 2.

We show, in Fig. 10, the diagram of the reaper tournament we have just explained.

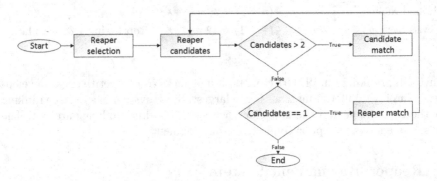

Fig. 10. The diagram of the reaper tournament system

4.2   Analysis of Reaper Tournament

We analyze the reaper tournament as done in the previous section.

Number of Matches: For a reaper tournament with 8 participants, there would be 15 to 17 matches. Since the pairing depends on who among the participants is the reaper, the total number of matches could be 15, 16 or 17. The minimum number of matches per participant is 2, and the maximum is 8.

For the reaper tournament with 4 participants, there would be exactly 5 matches, while for 16 participants it would consists of 39 to 47 matches or could be more. We have not found a general formula for the number of matches in the reaper tournament.

Competitiveness Development: Figure 11 shows the progress tree of the reaper tournament with 8 participants. Although the nodes for the reaper candidate vary depending on the actual progress, it is ensured that every win will lead to a shorter path toward higher value leaf nodes. Furthermore, the prizes are decided in bottom-up way, and all participants who are not eliminated have the chance to be awarded any remaining prize. Thus, the reaper tournament has no problem in competitiveness development.

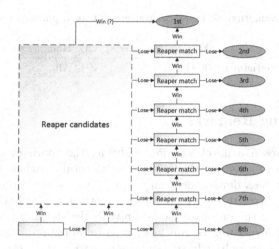

Fig. 11. Progress tree of the reaper tournament for 8 participants

Ranking Precision: We assume that we have 8 participants with credits numbers varying from 1 to 8, and the more credits always win the match. Table 11 shows the expected ranking outcome of the tournament and the actual results counting all $8! = 40320$ permutations.

Table 11. The expected and actual ranking of the reaper tournament for 8 participants

Participant	Expected ranking	Ranking precision
1	8th place	40320 (100%)
2	7th place	40320 (100%)
3	6th place	40320 (100%)
4	5th place	40320 (100%)
5	4th place	40320 (100%)
6	3rd place	40320 (100%)
7	2nd place	40320 (100%)
8	1st place	40320 (100%)

4.3   Evaluation

We show, in Table 12, the extended version of Table 10, with the reaper tournament added to the list. The reaper tournament successfully satisfies competitiveness development and provides convincing rankings for all participants. Furthermore, for 8 participants case, the number of matches required is just slightly larger than the classic double-elimination.

Table 12. Evaluation of the reaper tournament for n participants ($n = 8$)

System	Matches (for $n = 8$)	CD	Ranking precision
Reaper tournament	15–17	✓	All

5   Concluding Remarks

This paper proposed a novel way for analyzing the tournament systems. It focused on three aspects namely the number of total matches in the tournament, competitiveness development and ranking precision. It then proposed a notion of progress tree to detect potential unmotivated matches. The analysis we performed using the proposed method reveals the strength and weakness of each tournament structure. To conclude, single-elimination is best if we want to qualify one winner only. Classic double-elimination is a better choice if we want to qualify two top winners. Round-robin system provides reliable ranking precision for all participants. However, the number of matches is very high, and it fails to maintain competitiveness development. Swiss System can qualify the top winner and the last place, but its competitiveness development is poor.

Realizing that there currently is no tournament systems which could satisfy competitiveness development, we proposed a new tournament system called reaper tournament system. It is able to maintain competitiveness development while providing convincing rankings for all participants. However, we have not yet found a general formula for the number of matches. From our observation, the reaper tournament would have less number of matches than classic double-elimination in case with 4 participants, slightly larger in case with 8 players, and more in case with 16 players.

In future works, we plan to investigate the characteristics of the reaper tournament system. For example, finding out the general formula to calculate the maximum and minimum number of matches for a given number of participants.

Acknowledgment. We thank Dr. T. Takizawa for showing us the Swiss tournament system sample code, it was really helpful for our understanding.

References

1. algolist.net. Selection sort (java, c++)—algorithms and data structures (2015). http://www.algolist.net/Algorithms/Sorting/Selection_sort. Accessed 14 Aug 2015
2. Brejov, B.: Analyzing variants of shellsort. Inf. Process. Lett. **79**(5), 223–227 (2001)
3. Cormen, T.H., Leiserson, C.E., Rivest, R.L., Stein, C.: Introduction to Algorithms, 2nd edn. MIT Press, Cambridge (2001)
4. dota2.com. Main event - statitics - asia championships - dota2 (2015). http://dac.dota2.com.cn/statistical/main.htm. Accessed 12 Aug 2015
5. dota2.com. Dota 2 - the international (2016). http://www.dota2.com/international/replays/4/1/. Accessed 1 Feb 2017

6. Elo, A.: The Rating of Chess Players, Past and Present. Arco Publishing, New York (1975)
7. Han, Y.: Deterministic sorting in O (n log log n) time and linear space. J. Algorithms **50**(1), 96–105 (2004)
8. Han, Y., Thorup, M.: Integer sorting in O(n radic;(log log n)) expected time and linear space. In: Proceedings of the 43rd Annual IEEE Symposium on Foundations of Computer Science, pp. 135–144 (2002)
9. Kaiser, E., Feng, W.C.: Playerrating: a reputation system for multiplayer online games. In: 2009 8th Annual Workshop on Network and Systems Support for Games (NetGames), pp. 1–6, November 2009
10. Knuth, D.E.: The Art of Computer Programming: Sorting and Searching, vol. 3, 2nd edn. Addison Wesley Longman Publishing Co., Inc., Redwood City (1998)
11. Graepel, T., Herbrich, R., Minka, T.: Trueskill$^{(TM)}$: a Bayesian skill rating system. In: Advances in Neural Information Processing Systems, vol. 20, pp. 569–576. MIT Press, Cambridge, January 2007
12. Graepel, T., Herbrich, R., Minka, T.: Trueskill through time: revisiting the history of chess. In: Advances in Neural Information Processing Systems, vol. 20, pp. 931–938. MIT Press, Cambridge, January 2008
13. Sanderson, A.R., Siegfried, J.J.: Thinking about competitive balance. J. Sports Econ. **4**, 255–279 (2003)
14. Schmidt, M.B., Berri, D.J.: Competitive balance and attendance: the case of major league baseball. J. Sports Econ. **2**, 145–167 (2001)
15. Sedgewick, R.: Implementing quicksort programs. Commun. ACM **21**(10), 847–857 (1978)
16. Shim, K.J., Ahmad, M.A., Pathak, N., Srivastava, J.: Inferring player rating from performance data in massively multiplayer online role-playing games (MMORPGS). In: International Conference on Computational Science and Engineering, CSE 2009, vol. 4, pp. 1199–1204, August 2009
17. Sucar, L.E.: Graph theory. Probabilistic Graphical Models. ACVPR, pp. 27–38. Springer, London (2015). https://doi.org/10.1007/978-1-4471-6699-3_3
18. Szymanski, S.: Income inequality, competitive balance and the attractiveness of team sports: some evidence and a natural experiment from English soccer. Econ. J. **111**, 69–84 (2001). 108 Cowley, Oxford OX4 IJF, UK and 350 Main Street, Maiden, MA 20148, USA (2001). Blacwell Publisher
19. Thorup, M.: Randomized sorting in O(n log log n) time and linear space using addition, shift, and bit-wise boolean operations. J. Algorithms **42**(2), 205–230 (2002)
20. Zhang, L., Wu, J., Wang, Z.C., Wang, C.J.: A factor-based model for context-sensitive skill rating systems. In: 2010 22nd IEEE International Conference on Tools with Artificial Intelligence, vol. 2, pp. 249–255, October 2010

Analysis of Average Hand-Drawing and Its Application

Shinjiro Niino$^{(\boxtimes)}$, Nanae Hagiwara, Satoshi Nakamura,
Masaaki Suzuki, and Takanori Komatsu

Graduate School of Advanced Mathematical Sciences,
Meiji University, Tokyo, Japan
shinn070110@gmail.com

Abstract. In this paper, we applied averaging method to hand-drawn illustrations, and clarified characteristics of the averaged hand-drawings. We then implemented a prototype system that can realize better hand-drawings for user based on the characteristics.

Keywords: Hand drawing · Averaging · Comics · Illustrations · Drawing tool

1 Introduction

The opportunities for hand-drawing illustrations on a computer are increasing because of the spread of computers equipped with a pen-based interface, such as tablet PCs, and smartphones. In addition, the opportunities to share these illustrations with others are also increasing because of starting Web services for sharing user-generated illustrations such as pixiv [1].

However, some people do not like to draw illustrations even if they liked doing so in childhood. There are many reasons for this change in preference. One reason is that people are no longer satisfied with their hand-drawn illustrations because he/she hand-drawn illustrations tend to differ from their ideal shape and style. Here, the ideal shape and style of hand-drawn illustrations has not been clarified yet because people have trouble visualizing the image in their heads.

In our previous work, we designed a method to generate an average handwritten character from several handwritten characters by expressing users' strokes as equations [2]. In user-based experimental tests, we clarified that the average handwritten Japanese Hiragana characters were more beautiful than the original handwritten characters. Thus, the average handwritten Japanese Hiragana characters are similar to their ideal shape and style. We guess that the characteristics of the average hand-drawn illustration are similar to the average handwritten Japanese Hiragana characters.

In this work, we first clarify the characteristics of the average hand-drawn illustrations and the ideal image. Here, we make two hypotheses about the average hand-drawn illustrations and ideal image of users:

- A user's average illustrations are more beautiful than his/her hand-drawn illustrations (Hypothesis 1).

© ICST Institute for Computer Sciences, Social Informatics and Telecommunications Engineering 2018
Y. Chisik et al. (Eds.): INTETAIN 2017, LNICST 215, pp. 34–48, 2018.
https://doi.org/10.1007/978-3-319-73062-2_3

- The average illustrations of several users are more beautiful than each user's average illustrations (Hypothesis 2).

  Here, if averaging illustrations reproduce the ideal illustration, the illustrations would not change in either case of dominant hand or non-dominant hand. Thus, we make hypothesis:

- The average non-dominant-hand illustrations become similar to the average dominant-hand illustrations (Hypothesis 3).

We test these hypotheses by conducting evaluation experiments. If the average illustrations are valued by users, these average illustrations might be similar to the ideal image. In addition, if the average non-dominant-hand illustration is similar to the average dominant-hand illustrations, the averaged illustrations might be the ideal for the user.

Thus, we implement a prototype system to help users to hand-draw illustrations on the basis of the characteristics of the average hand-drawn illustrations clarified in this work and the ideal image of the user's hand drawing. In addition, we herein discuss the usefulness of our system.

2   Related Work

There are many studies to support hand-drawing by showing guides or examples. ShadowDraw [3] is a system that shows the drawing guide of a user's target illustration as shadow images in the background on a canvas on the basis of numerous illustrations while a user is drawing. In addition, DrawFromDrawings [4] is a system that supports users to hand-draw their illustration by using large illustration databases. In this method, a user firstly hand-draw an illustration and specify a part of the illustration in order to improve from the illustration database and can select a target model from illustration database to merge a part of his/her stroke and a part of model depending on the user's operation. These systems enable users to hand-draw illustrations easily.

There are many methods to beautify strokes in hand-drawn illustrations based on knowledge or large database. Pegasus [5] is a system to help users to draw geometric diagrams. This helps users to easily draw difficult illustrations such as parallelograms or experimental apparatus. Limpaecher et al. [6] proposed a method that adjusted users' blurry strokes in real-time by finding a consensus stroke generated from a crowd-sourced large collection of hand-drawn illustrations with mobile application. In addition, Zitnick [7] proposed a method that beautified hand-drawn strokes by calculating a curvature of strokes and averaging the curvature with user's previous stroke. An objective of our work is to clarify the characteristics of beautification by averaging hand-drawings. We believe that our results assist these methods.

dePENd [8] is an assist system for hand-drawing physically. This system controls movement of user's sketch by using ferromagnetism of a ballpoint pen and their desk-type device set actuator with magnet. That allows user to draw difficult diagrams and pictures consisting of lines and circles. If we apply our averaging method to this system, users may be able to hand-draw beautiful averaging stroke easily.

In our previous work, we proposed a method to practice hand-drawing illustration [9] based on averaging method [2]. The method merges a user's stroke and model's stroke dynamically depending on the specified merge rate, and increase the user's motivation because he/she can hand-draw more beautiful illustration than his/her skill. This work is one of the application based on our knowledge.

3 Averaging Method

An illustration consists of several strokes. Then, the averaging method [2] generates a mathematical expression for each stroke and generates its average stroke from corresponding strokes by using arithmetic calculations. Thus, the method makes an average illustration by combining these average strokes.

First, the method enables users to draw on a canvas and obtains all of the users' strokes as a series of points. Then, the method interpolates intervals between these points by using spline interpolation. After that, the method generates a mathematical expression for each stroke through all interpolated points by using the Fourier series expansion (Fig. 1).

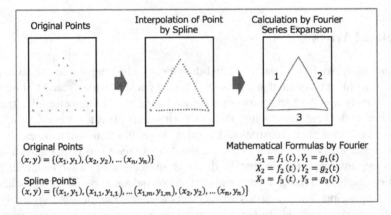

Fig. 1. Method of generating mathematical formulas of hand-drawn illustrations.

A stroke is expressed by a parametric representation as

$$\begin{cases} x = f(t) \\ y = g(t) \end{cases} - \pi \le t \le \pi. \tag{1}$$

Here, the method doubles back the interpolated points at the end of the points because the series of points has to be a closed curve in order to use the Fourier series expansion. If a distance exists between the start and end points, the ends of a particular stroke become wavy because both ends are connected by the Fourier series expansion. Although $f(t)$ is not a periodic function, it can be considered as a periodic function by the following definition ($g(t)$ is the same as $f(t)$)

$$f(t) = f(t + 2n\pi) \qquad n : integer. \tag{2}$$

Furthermore, $f(t)$ can be expressed using the Fourier series expansion as follows

$$f(t) = \frac{a_0}{2} + \sum_{n=1}^{\infty}(a_n \cos nt + b_n \sin nt). \tag{3}$$

a_n and b_n can be calculated as follows

$$\begin{cases} a_n = \frac{1}{\pi}\int_{-\pi}^{\pi}f(t) \cdot \cos nt\, dt \\ b_n = \frac{1}{\pi}\int_{-\pi}^{\pi}f(t) \cdot \sin nt\, dt \end{cases} \tag{4}$$

Here, interpolated points are discrete data. Therefore, we calculate the approximate a_n and b_n by summing these data.

However, computers cannot use an infinite series of a mathematical expressions. Therefore, the method truncates it to degree n places by comparing the distance between n series and $n + 1$ series with a threshold, which we set 2px in this paper.

As a result, the i_{th} hand-drawn stroke is expressed as $(x, y) = (f_i(t), g_i(t))$. The method generates the average stroke from N strokes as follows

$$\begin{cases} x_i = \frac{1}{N}\sum_{k=1}^{N}f_{i,k}(t) \\ \qquad\qquad\qquad\qquad 0 \le t \le \pi. \\ y_i = \frac{1}{N}\sum_{k=1}^{N}g_{i,k}(t) \end{cases} \tag{5}$$

The method displays the average stroke by changing the value t from 0 to π, since the rest half also shows the same stroke in the opposite direction.

4 Dataset for Illustrations

We created a dataset of hand-drawn illustrations to test our hypotheses.

4.1 System of Creating Dataset

The system of creating datasets was implemented by Processing, programming language. Figure 1 shows this system. The system shows what kind of character the user should hand-draw, how many strokes the user hand-draw, the progress of creating the dataset, the "Undo" button, "Next" button, and the canvas for hand-drawing.

First, a user types his/her name. At the same time, the system automatically makes the user a folder in which to save his/her illustration data. After that, the screen changes the appearance, as shown in Fig. 2. The screen is W520px × H600px, and the hand-drawing canvas is W500px × H500px.

When a user is drawing a stroke by hand inside this canvas field by using a stylus, the stroke is displayed as a series of points in red (see left of Fig. 2). Our system obtains and plots 60 points per second (60 fps). When the user releases the stylus from the surface of the display, the system connects each continuous point with a line and displays them in blue (see right of Fig. 2). The system ignores the user's input when it

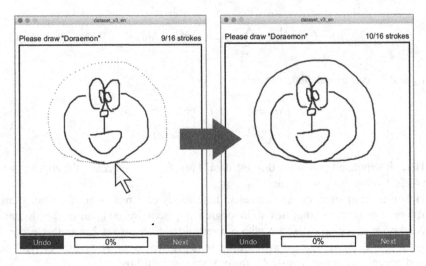

Fig. 2. Screen snapshot of system for generating datasets of hand-drawn illustrations. (Color figure online)

draws a stroke outside of this canvas. The user can remove previous hand-drawn strokes by clicking "Undo." When the user finishes drawing the target illustration and clicks "Next," the system refreshes the canvas field and displays the name of the next target illustration. At the same time, the system automatically saves the hand-drawn data, which contain x- and y-coordinates of the points of the strokes, and saves the illustration as a PNG image.

In this paper, we selected four hand-drawn illustrations of characters well known in Japan for the target illustrations: Doraemon (©Fujiko-Pro, Shogakukan, TV-Asahi, Shin-ei, and ADK), Anpanman (©Yanase・F・T・H ©APDLLP), Baikinman (©Yanase・F・T・H ©APDLLP), and Cook San. In addition, we prepared instruction Web pages consisting of images of illustrations and the stroke order and the stroke direction (Fig. 3).

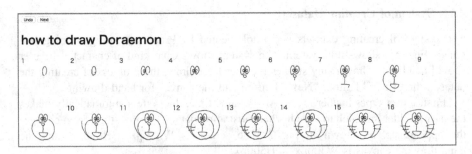

Fig. 3. Web page showing how to hand-draw Doraemon.

In creating the dataset, we asked eight users to hand-draw four illustrations following the stroke order and the stroke direction showed by the Web page in order to generate average hand-drawn illustrations using our method.

Here, users are undergraduate students in Meiji University, 20–22 years old, seven right-handed persons and one left-handed person, and four men and four women. None of the students had professional level talent at drawing. They drew each illustration five times using their dominant hand and then five times using their non-dominant hand.

We prepared CINTIQ 13HD produced by Wacom as an input interface. In addition, we used Apple MacBook Pro (Retina 13-inch Processor 2.8 GHz Inter Core i5 Memory 16 GB 16 MHz DDR3) computers to run this system.

4.2 Average Illustrations

We generated images of the hand-drawn illustrations and the average hand-drawn illustrations from the dataset. After that, we generated the following illustrations for each target character. Figures 4 and 5 shows an example. In this, there are 428 images generated by our method.

- Each user's original illustrations drawn using the dominant hand:

$$(4\,characters \times 8\,users \times 5\,times = 160\,patterns)$$

- Each user's original illustrations drawn using the non-dominant hand:

$$(4\,characters \times 8\,users \times 5\,times = 160\,patterns)$$

- Each user's average illustrations drawn using the dominant hand:

$$(4\,characters \times 8\,users = 32\,patterns)$$

- Each user's average illustrations drawn using the non-dominant hand:

$$(4\,characters \times 8\,users = 32\,patterns)$$

- Each user's average illustrations drawn using both hands:

$$(4\,characters \times 8\,users = 32\,patterns)$$

- All users' average illustrations drawn using the dominant hand:

$$(4\,characters = 4\,patterns)$$

- All users' average illustrations drawn using the non-dominant hand:

$$(4\,characters = 4\,patterns)$$

- All users' average illustrations drawn using both hands:

$$(4\,characters = 4\,patterns)$$

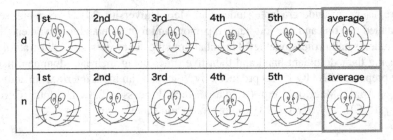

Fig. 4. User's hand-drawn Doraemon and averaged Doraemon ('d' stand for dominant hand and 'n' stand for non-dominant hand)

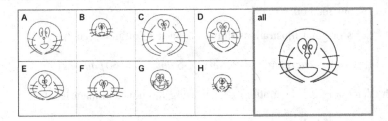

Fig. 5. Each user's average Doraemon and all users' average Doraemon.

5 Evaluation Experiment

To test the three hypotheses described in the above, we implemented a web-based experiment system (Figs. 6 and 9) and 16 undergrads (14 men and 4 women; 20–22 years old) were participated. These participants were asked to evaluate illustrations generated from the dataset by this system. In this experiment, eight participants of them contributed to generate the dataset. We conducted following experiments for each hypothesis.

5.1 Experiment1

5.1.1 Procedure
In this experiment, we compare participant's average illustrations with participant's original illustrations. We asked participants to rank the first, second and third best illustrations from 13 patterns (four dominant-hand's and four non-dominant-hand's original illustrations, and average illustrations by dominant-hand and by non-dominant, and the average of both hands) depending on the degree of beauty in each target character and in each user (see Fig. 6). They rank illustrations 32 times ($= 8\,users \times 4\,illustrations.$)

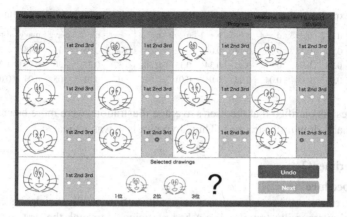

Fig. 6. Web system for experimental test to rank illustrations.

5.1.2   Result

Figure 7 and Table 1 shows the results of experiment 1. In this figure, 'd' stands for the dominant hand, 'n' the non-dominant hand, and 'avg' the averaged illustrations.

In Fig. 7, the horizontal axis shows the first to fifth dominant-hand illustrations, first to fifth non-dominant-hand illustrations, and the averaged dominant-hand, non-dominant-hand, and both-hand illustrations. Here, we assigned three points to first ranked illustrations, two to second ranked ones, and one to third ranked ones. The evaluation score was the average value of these points. The expected value for one illustration was 0.4615 because the sum value of scores was 6.

Figure 7 shows the averaged illustrations were evaluated higher than the original hand-drawn illustrations. Furthermore, the averaged illustrations drawn using both hands had the highest score.

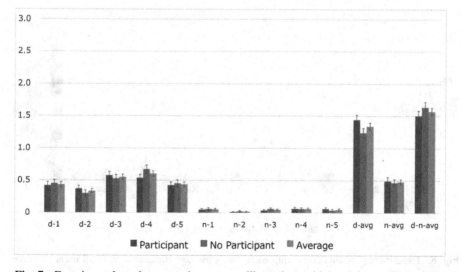

Fig. 7. Experimental results comparing average illustrations with hand-drawn illustrations.

Table 1. Experimental results comparing average illustrations with hand-drawn illustrations.

	d − 1	d − 2	d − 3	d − 4	d − 5	n − 1	n − 2	n − 3	n − 4	n − 5	d-avg	n-avg	d-n-avg
AVG	0.43	0.33	0.55	0.60	0.44	0.05	0.02	0.05	0.06	0.05	1.35	0.48	1.58
SD	0.90	0.78	0.96	0.97	0.85	0.34	0.17	0.30	0.37	0.32	1.20	0.90	1.26
SE	0.04	0.03	0.04	0.04	0.04	0.01	0.01	0.01	0.02	0.01	0.05	0.04	0.06

These results clarified that the user's average illustrations were more beautiful than the user's hand-drawn illustrations. Thus, hypothesis 1 was validated.

5.2 Experiment2

5.2.1 Procedure

In this experiment, we compare the average illustration of all participants and each participants' average illustrations. We asked participants to rank the first, second and third best illustrations from nine patterns (the average illustration of eight participants and eight participants' average illustration) depending on the degree of beauty in each target character and in each hand (see Fig. 6). They rank illustrations 12 times ($= 4\,characters \times 3\,hands.$)

5.2.2 Result

Figure 8 and Table 2 shows the results of experiment 2.

This figure shows the evaluation scores for A's to H's averaged illustrations and the average illustrations by all users. Here, we again assigned three, two, and one points to the first, second, and third ranked illustrations. The evaluation score was the average value of these points, so the expected value for one illustration was again 0.4615 because the sum value of scores was 6.

Figure 8 shows all users' average illustrations were evaluated higher than each user's average illustrations.

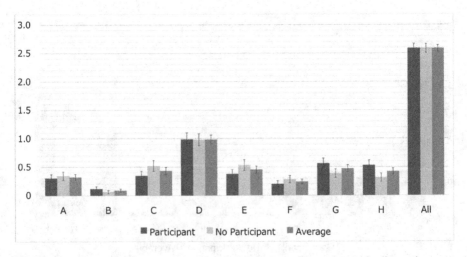

Fig. 8. Experimental results comparing each user's average illustration with all users' average illustrations.

Table 2. Experimental results comparing each user's average illustration with all users' average illustrations.

	A	B	C	D	E	F	G	H	All
AVG	0.32	0.09	0.43	0.98	0.45	0.24	0.47	0.42	2.58
SD	0.68	0.36	0.87	1.06	0.85	0.58	0.82	0.78	0.77
SE	0.05	0.03	0.06	0.08	0.06	0.04	0.06	0.06	0.06

These results clarified that all the users' average illustrations were more beautiful than each user's ones. Thus, hypothesis 2 was validated. We suppose that these results mean that averaging illustrations cancels out each person's blurry hand drawings by moving them toward ideal illustrations.

5.3 Experiment3

5.3.1 Procedure

In this experiment, we check how similar dominant-hand's illustration and non-dominant-hand's illustration based on participants' evaluation. We asked participants to pair each user's average dominant-hand illustration and each user's non-dominant-hand illustration depending on the similarity (see Fig. 9). They rank illustrations four times ($= 4\,characters.$)

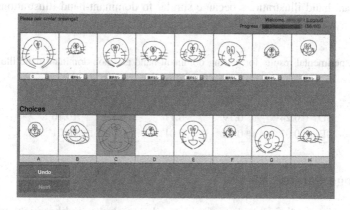

Fig. 9. Web system to pair dominant-hand and non-dominant–hand illustrations.

5.3.2 Result

Figure 10 and Table 3 shows the results of experiment 3.

This figure shows the percentages of correct pairings of dominant-hand and non-dominant-hand illustrations. The expected percentage of correct pairings was 13%.

Figure 10 shows the percentage of correct answers was more than 70% for all illustrations. This means that the dominant-hand illustrations were similar to the non-dominant-hand illustrations.

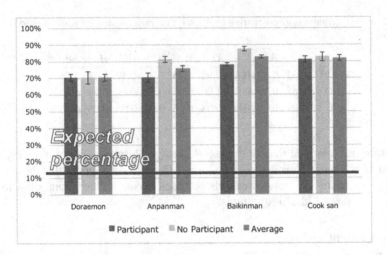

Fig. 10. Experimental results for pairing dominant-hand and non-dominant-hand illustrations.

We think there are two reasons for this. First, the blurred non-dominant-hand illustrations were made more beautiful by averaging them. Second, the averaged illustrations kept their hand-drawn traits regardless of whether the dominant or non-dominant hand was used. These results clarified that the average non-dominant-hand illustrations became similar to dominant-hand illustrations. Thus, hypothesis 3 was validated (Table 3).

Table 3. Experimental results for pairing dominant-hand and non-dominant-hand illustrations.

	Doraemon	Anpanman	Baikinman	Cook San	Average
AVG	0.70	0.76	0.83	0.82	0.78
SD	0.24	0.19	0.11	0.18	0.10
SE	0.02	0.02	0.01	0.02	0.01

6 Average Painter

When a user is unsatisfied with his/her hand-drawn stroke, he/she might undo that stroke and redraw it. Here, we clarified the average illustrations were more beautiful than individual hand-drawn illustrations (Hypothesis 1). In fact, the user was able to draw beautiful strokes if the system automatically generated the average stroke from these redrawn strokes.

To realize such drawings, we introduce a beautifying function based on averaging strokes to painting software (Fig. 11). This function is based on the users' behaviors and Hypothesis 1 and works as follows:

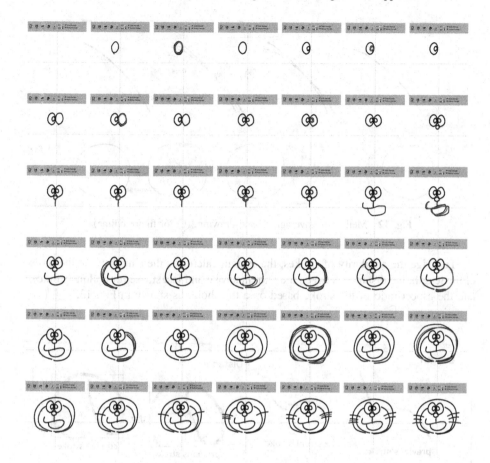

Fig. 11. Screen shot of "Average Painter" system.

- When a user draws a stroke, undoes the stroke, and redraws a stroke similar to the undone stroke, the function generates an average stroke from the undone stroke and redrawn stroke in order to beautify his/her drawings.
- When a user draws a stroke and redraws a stroke similar to the last stroke, the function generates an average stroke from these two strokes in order to beautify his/her drawings.

In this study, we implemented a prototype of the drawing system "Average Painter" with this function by processing to assist users in hand-drawing illustrations.

This system automatically shows the candidate of a user's ideal stroke by averaging the current stroke and last stroke or by averaging the current stroke and undone stroke.

This system automatically shows the candidate stroke in red if the system judges that a user's current stroke is similar to his/her last stroke or undone stroke. If the user clicks this candidate stroke, the system deletes the current stroke and last stroke and shows the average stroke as his/her hand-drawn stroke (Fig. 12).

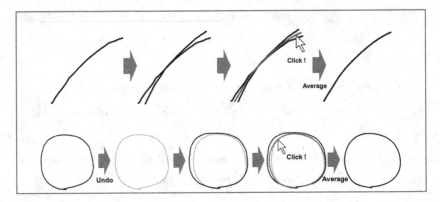

Fig. 12. Method for averaging hand-drawing. (Color figure online)

To judge the similarity of strokes, the system calculates the similarity on the basis of the length, the distance between the current stroke and last stroke (or undone stroke), and the aspect ratio of the stroke based on a threshold, as shown in Fig. 13.

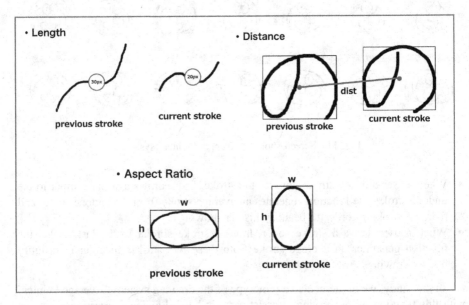

Fig. 13. The similarity is calculated by using the difference of length, distance, and aspect ratio of each stroke.

We demonstrated our system to many participants and asked them to try using it to hand-draw illustrations. We were told in feedback that if the user was unsatisfied with the hand-drawn stroke, the stroke became more beautiful by using the averaging function. Thus, the user was satisfied with his/her hand-drawing when our system assisted him/her.

However, several participants reported that they could not draw complex strokes smoothly. In the future, we will solve this problem by fixing software bugs.

Figure 14 shows examples of illustrations, which three participants draw without the averaging function and with that as users like. They are students in Meiji University and their age is 22. In this test, we showed the model's characters, and asked three participants to draw the character with our system and without our system. After that, we got feedback from them. They said "I could draw more beautiful illustration with average function than drawing by one time" or "I was hard to draw whisker by being shown average stroke with average function."

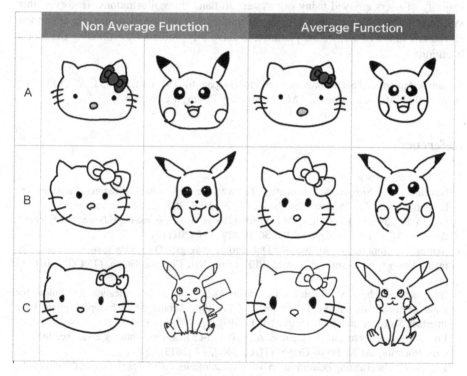

Fig. 14. Example of illustrations by using Average Painter system.

7   Conclusion and Future Tasks

In this paper, we made three hypotheses about hand-drawing illustrations.

- A user's average illustrations are more beautiful than his/her hand-drawn illustrations
- The average illustrations of users are more beautiful than each user's average illustrations
- The average non-dominant hand illustrations become similar to the average dominant hand illustrations

Then, we described an averaging method, our collection of four types of hand-drawn illustrations, and some experiments we conducted to test these hypotheses. The experimental results verified the hypotheses.

In the experiments, we required users to keep to the stroke order and direction of illustration. Some users had difficulty drawing illustrations, so we will implement an averaging system to sort hand-drawn strokes automatically in the future. If we use such a system, the results should become more accurate because users would be able to draw more easily.

In addition, we implemented a prototype system of a drawing tool for assisting with hand-drawing by using an averaging method based on hypothesis 1. As a result, the majority of users enjoyed using our system to hand draw illustrations. However, this system is not suitable for illustrations requiring many strokes such as the hair of cartoon characters. In the future, we are planning to solve this problem by estimating the user's intentions.

Acknowledgments. This work was supported in part by JST CREST, JST ACCEL Grant Number JPMJAC1602, Japan, and Meiji University Priority Research A.

References

1. pixiv. http://www.pixiv.net/
2. Nakamura, S., Suzuki, M., Komatsu, T.: Average handwritten Hiragana-characters are beautiful. Trans. Inf. Process. Soc. Japan **52**(12), 2599–2609 (2016). (in Japanese)
3. Lee, Y.J., Zitnick, L., Cohen, M.: ShadowDraw: real-time user guidance for freehand drawing. ACM Trans. Graph. (TOG) **30**(4), 879–887 (2011)
4. Matsui, Y., Shiratori, T., Aizawa, K.: DrawFromDrawings: 2D drawing assistance via stroke interpolation with a sketch database. IEEE Trans. Vis. Comput. Graph. (TVCG) (2016, in press)
5. Igarashi, T., Sachiko, K., Hidehiko, T., Satoshi, M.: Interactive beautification: a technique for rapid geometric design. In: Proceedings of the 10th Annual ACM Symposium on User Interface Software and Technology (UIST 1997), pp. 105–114 (1997)
6. Limpaecher, A., Feltman, N., Treuille, A., Cohen, M.: Real-time drawing assistance through crowdsourcing. ACM Trans. Graph. (TOG) **30**(4), 54 (2013)
7. Zitnick, L.: Handwriting beautification using token means. ACM Trans. Graph. (TOG) **32**(4), 53 (2013)
8. Yamaoka, J., Kakehi, Y.: dePENd: augmented handwriting sketching system using ferromagnetism of a ballpoint pen. In: Proceedings of the 26th Annual ACM Symposium on User Interface Software and Technology (UIST 2013), pp. 203–210 (2013)
9. Kubota, N., Niino, S., Nakamura, S., Suzuki, M.: A sustainable practice method of hand-drawing by merging user's stroke and model's stroke. In: The First International Workshop on coMics ANalysis, Processing and Understanding (MANPU 2016), no. 10, pp. 1–6 (2016)

Dynamorph: Montessori Inspired Design for Seniors with Dementia Living in Long-Term Care Facilities

Yuan Feng[1,2(✉)], Ruud van Reijmersdal[2], Suihuai Yu[1(✉)], Matthias Rauterberg[2], Jun Hu[2], and Emilia Barakova[2]

[1] Department of Industrial Design, Northwestern Polytechnical University, Xi'an, People's Republic of China
Y.Feng@tue.nl, ysuihuai@vip.sina.com
[2] Department of Industrial Design, Eindhoven University of Technology, Eindhoven, The Netherlands
r.j.h.v.reijmersdal@student.tue.nl,
{g.w.m.rauterberg, j.hu, e.i.Barakova}@tue.nl

Abstract. Seniors with dementia living in nursing homes are often faced with boredom and loneliness due to lack of meaningful engagement and personalized activities. We applied Montessori method to design an interactive table for elderly home residents and evaluated the design with four female residents and a nurse. This method offers a range of levelled interactions to meet the needs at different stages and cognitive decline levels of the residents with dementia. The table initiates interaction with an increasing level of complexity that magnifies the rewarding effects and social connectedness among the residents. The qualitative evaluation during a pilot study indicated that the interactions with the table reduced agitation of the elderly participants and increased the instances of positive social behaviours.

Keywords: Dementia · Interaction design · Montessori method
Long-term care · Nursing home

1 Introduction

Dementia is a global problem that affects 47.5 million people and each year 7.7 million new cases are reported [1]. The symptoms of dementia are a decline of cognitive function, language abilities, mobility and memory loss, and varies with every individual. Although the progress can be slow, from months to years or decades, it will severely influence one's ability to live an independent life. Therefore, patients need help from informal caregivers or, more often, care facilities. In dementia nursing homes, residents often suffer from lack of activity and stimulation [2], which could result in boredom [3], agitation or other discomforts [4]. Engagement is defined as 'the act of being occupied or involved with an external stimulus' by Cohen-Mansfield [5]. It proves to have a positive effect as it decreases boredom or agitation. During the past decades, different kinds of non-pharmacological interventions for dementia have been studied in order to provide adequate stimulation [6]. However, limited by the number

© ICST Institute for Computer Sciences, Social Informatics and Telecommunications Engineering 2018
Y. Chisik et al. (Eds.): INTETAIN 2017, LNICST 215, pp. 49–58, 2018.
https://doi.org/10.1007/978-3-319-73062-2_4

of qualified personnel and by implementation difficulties, interventions often took place in a group without considering the personal conditions of seniors with dementia.

Customized or personalized stimulations and activities based on the cognitive level or the personal experiences of dementia patients proved can decrease agitation and dementia related problematic behaviour significantly [7–9]. An example of such applications is *CIRCA* [10]. *CIRCA* is a touch screen based interaction that uses video, music, pictures and text to help persons with dementia and their caregivers to have more personalised and engaging conversations. Tailored Activity Program (*TAP*) [11] is another example of customized activity for dementia patients. The program aims to identify interests and capabilities of persons with dementia, and developed occupational therapy intervention especially tailored for individual profiles to reduce some unwanted behavioural symptoms. Due to decreasing cognitive functions of individuals with dementia, related research suggests that being active can enhance social connectedness, the consistency of self-identity, bring positive affections and decrease frustrations [12, 13]. Meaningful activities for nursing home residents with dementia was shown to reduce agitation, decrease behavioural problems, and enhance the quality of life [14].

In this paper, we present *Dynamorph*, a Montessori method inspired interactive table designed for seniors with dementia living in long-term care facilities. *Dynamorph* aims to help users minimize boredom, reduce agitation, generate connectedness and make a positive impact with minimal involvement of the nurses, by providing the right amount of stimulations and meaningful activities.

2   Montessori Method

The Montessori method was originally developed by Maria Montessori while working with mentally challenged children [15]. Later on, this educational method has been widely adopted to teach cognitive, social and functional skills to children. It breaks down tasks into steps from simple to complex, from concrete to abstract, making students move only a little beyond their comfort zone whilst preserving the ability to improve. The same principle was later applied to persons with dementia by Camp [16] and showed that Montessori activities are well suited for dementia groups as well.

Dynamorph utilizes the Montessori method for designing activities that suit personal profiles of residents with dementia. For instance, puzzling is identified as a common activity for residents with dementia in nursing homes. However, due to the decline of their cognitive functions, seniors often face frustration caused by not succeeding in completing the puzzle. Therefore, puzzling showed to have few positive effects. We argue that Montessori method, instead, can better offer activities that reflect the individuals' interests and skill levels [17], because it is based on levelled framework that breaks the interaction into steps and processes that range from simple to complex, and from concrete to abstract. Seniors can freely explore and the caregivers can control the interaction levels in order to fit different users' conditions and a range of needs.

3 Design of *Dynamorph*

3.1 Concept

Adopting essential elements from the Montessori educational method such as self-exploration, task break down, rewarding system, tangible interactions [16, 18, 19], *Dynamorph* was designed to provide meaningful activities suited for the personal conditions of the seniors. In addition, the table was designed to fit the daily routines of the seniors, requiring only minimal involvement of nurses. Following an iterative design process, caregivers and residents with dementia were involved within the development of *Dynamorph*, a table with multi-layered interactive interfaces (Fig. 1).

Fig. 1. The final prototype of the *Dynamorph*.

The tangible interfaces are composed of two basic elements: four zoomorphic shapes on each sitting place of the table and four leaf-like shapes pointing to the centre of the table. The zoomorphic shapes are made of attractive, vibrant coloured goose down with a soft sponge core consisting of ball sets inside. The size of the core is designed to ensure comfortable grasping so that the seniors can squeeze and hold these artefacts, and the down offers cheerful appearance, invites touch, and adds some animal fur feeling to it. Each zoomorphic shape consists of three individual balls mounted on different motors that visually appear like a single entity and are programmed to mimic several animal-like movements (Fig. 2(a)). For example, if all three balls slowly move up and down in different directions, they appear alive, pulsing and breathing. The illusion of a single entity suggests a natural and animal-like character.

Each organic leaf shape was made with transparent acrylic-based resin plate. The leaves were milled to be hollow so that they could be filled up with coloured liquid originating from each ball set, forming together as a connected pattern. If a senior interacts with a zoomorphic shape this will be detected by conductive wires hidden in the balls. The heart rate sensors installed besides the ball set on the table would pick up the signals detected from the wrists of the user, then transformed into dynamic leaf-shaped patterns filled by coloured liquid with the rhythm of the heartbeat, shown on the transparent surface of the table centre (Fig. 2(b)).

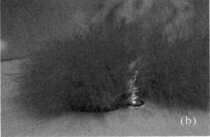

Fig. 2. The design details of *Dynamorph*. (a) Zoomorphic shapes consisting of three separate balls are mounted individually on mechanisms underneath the table to be programmed to respond correspondingly to user's gestures. (b) A zoomorphic shape powered by the interactive ball set with a pulse sensor embedded in the table.

3.2   Four-Layer Interaction Design Inspired by Montessori Method

Four-layer interaction structure was designed to alleviate boredom, bring connected-ness and further generate positive effects. Each layer has a specific meaning and embodies a hypothesis for potentially positive effects on the seniors with dementia.

In the first layer, interaction between individual and the zoomorphic object that pops out from the table takes place. The zoomorphic objects consist of sets of 3 balls that can be sensed under the feathers. This choice was made because related research indicated that the ball-shaped object is appealing to dementia patients with all levels of cognitive impairment [14]. The interactive ball sets were stitched with conductive wires then programmed to be able to sense the contact and force with which they are handled to distinguish different gestures. The reactions to different inputs are designed to perform as natural as possible and to adapt to the interacting person [20].

With the aim to provoke reactions from the senior person, one of the balls embedded in the zoomorphic shape starts popping out of table every 10 min, then dives back and pops up again with a higher altitude than before. Letting the ball dive faster than it rises creates a curious and bashful character. If this movement is ignored, the ball will slowly go back to the table through a hole and the zoomorphic shape will appear like a sad animal that did not get any attention. Then, 10 min later, another ball will come up and start a new loop of interaction. During the process, if the zoomorphic shape gets gently touched, held or petted, it will start to mimic the breathing pattern of an animal in order to give users a feeling of a pet. If it gets hit or slapped, the 'hurt' zoomorphic shape will hide in the table with a relatively high speed to show rejection towards user's behaviour. The attractiveness, designed movement and generated interactions of the zoomorphic shape form the first layer of interaction of *Dynamorph*.

The second layer aims to promote interaction between the individual and the leaf-shaped interface. Inspired by organic shapes, the pattern in the centre of the table was designed to be symmetrical and have aesthetic attributes. The pattern is normally transparent and therefore barely visible. It will appear in colour only when there is a continuous positive interaction with the corresponding zoomorphic shape, by filling up with coloured liquid in synchrony with the users' heartbeat signals. This behaviour was designed with the intention to give the user a sense of self-identity, as the self-identity stimulation is related to significantly higher levels of pleasure than other control stimulation within advanced stage dementia [12]. The use of liquid and organic shapes is also intended to have a calming effect, in order to ease agitated behaviours and enhance the positive engagement.

The third layer contains interactions among different modularized designs, which are intended to have an impact on self-awareness of the individual users [21]. Each ball set and the connected leaf-shaped pattern with liquid in its route were designed using cohesive colour choice with high contrast to enhance the attractiveness, keeps users' attention and give them a personal playing role as well [22]. It helps build a logic connection between the interactive ball sets and the patterns filled up with same coloured liquid. The liquid, instead of projection or lighting, is adopted in addition to a sound effect, as pumping with the heartbeat may sound like a rhythm and help users better recognize the feedback [23]. This modularized design aims to stimulate the self-awareness, and gives the seniors possibilities to make comparisons, so they are in charge of their own autonomy in controlling one set of the elements. Further fulfilling their need of controlling and possessing their own things, and may even generate the feeling of connectedness between nearby users.

The fourth layer attempts to stimulate interaction within the user group. When multiple users interacting with the ball sets trigger the corresponding liquid pumps, the centre area of the table will morph into a pattern with symmetric leaf shapes and different colours that are designed to be attractive. Creating the attractive pattern together would incur a sense of connectedness within the group. These four layers of interactions together form the four-layer interaction framework of *Dynamorph* (Fig. 3).

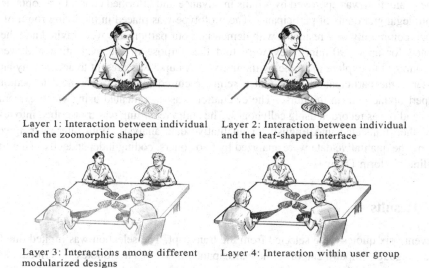

Layer 1: Interaction between individual   Layer 2: Interaction between individual
and the zoomorphic shape   and the leaf-shaped interface

Layer 3: Interactions among different   Layer 4: Interaction within user group
modularized designs

Fig. 3. Illustration of the four-layer interaction framework of *Dynamorph*.

4 Evaluation

4.1 Participants

Participants were recruited from Vitalis (KleinschaligWonen), Eindhoven, the Netherlands, an elderly care home that focuses on formal care for seniors with various forms and stages of dementia. The evaluation was conducted with four participants and one nurse for her expert feedback. The participants were all female, Dutch, with the average age of 85, ranging from 75 to 93. All the participants had the formal diagnosis of dementia and with different levels of cognitive decline according to the altered four-stage Clinical Dementia Rating Scale used in Vitalis. All participants are female due to the majority of residents being females (38 out of 40). Participants with a functioning level of auditory and visual abilities were selected. Participant demographics are presented in Table 1.

Table 1. Participant demographics.

Participant	Gender	Age	Stage	Form of dementia	Marriage status
P1	Female	75	2	Vascular dementia	Widowed
P2	Female	84	2–3	Vascular dementia	Married
P3	Female	88	2–3	Vascular dementia	Widowed
P4	Female	93	3	Vascular dementia	Widowed

4.2 Procedure

The evaluation was approved by Vitalis in advance and informed consent was obtained from legal guardians of participants. The prototype was placed in the living room of a small community of 7 residents with dementia. Four participants were invited and then seated for up to 90 min. They were told the purpose of the evaluation and were encouraged to explore the table by themselves. A nurse was present to accompany and observe the participants. After that a semi-structured interview was held to acquire expert opinions from the nurse. The evaluation was documented using video cameras and audio was recorded using cellphones. The audio recording was transcribed into text and then translated into English for qualitative data analysis. With inter-rater agreement, the qualitative data were analyzed by two coders, coding independently using the online platform Dedoose[1].

5 Results

Seventy six quotes were selected from the transcript. The selection was limited due to the language impairment of some participants. The selected quotes described their attitude towards the design and the interaction during the evaluation process. Resulting

---

[1] Online Dedoose platform for qualitative data analysis, www.dedoose.com.

from the process of collaborative coding, six categories of discussion themes emerged, as an indication of their focused interest points with subcategories and each subcategory with an exemplar quote, shown in Table 2.

Table 2. Categorization of discussion themes resulted from qualitative analysis, sub-categories, exemplars and number of quotes in each category/subcategories, the categories also reflect relationships correspond to four-layer interaction framework of *Dynamorph*.

Category of discussion themes	Correspond to interaction framework of *Dynamorph*	Sub-category	Exemplar quote
Interactive ball sets (43)	Layer 1	Aliveness (29)	"Look at this, it becomes alive. Look at this. Hello? (to the ball)" (P3)
		Aesthetics (14)	"Beautiful, wonderful, yes! That's very beautiful isn't it?" (P3)
Leaf-shaped pattern (7)	Layer 2	Leaf shapes (3)	"This is very beautiful (pointing to the leaf shape)." (P1)
		'River' (4)	"They are all swimming (referring to the colour liquid). It went all to this (draining by the outfall)." (P4)
Reflection of self-identity (8)	Layer 3	'My, mine' (5)	"Mine is moving, mine is alive. This one is working, and this one is not working anymore." (P3)
		Projection of one's heartbeat (3)	"It does only work for you, not for me, how is that possible? I don't have enough heart beat." (P1)
Social inclusion (9)	Layer 4	Forming a conversation (6)	"Don't you like it? (asking P2), there are beautiful things attached. Don't you think it's beautiful? (asking P2)" (P3)
		Instructing others (3)	"See? You play it like this, you can touch it (instructing P4)." (P3)
Emotion status (7)	–	Positive emotion feedback (5)	"It's cozy, we are cozy. I haven't had this for years." (P2)
		Making jokes (2)	"There might be a little guy in it." (P3)
Others (2)	–	Sharing past experience (1)	"This is beautiful. It is nice if you sew it somewhere else. I always sew, but nothing like this." (P1)
		Counting movements (1)	"Step, step, step. One, two, three ..." (P4)

During the evaluation, participants showed great interests toward the zoomorphic object that consisted of feather ball sets. The seniors interacted with those on own initiative and without any instruction. This shows that the concept worked quite well as an occupational engagement tool. Discussions around the interactive ball sets about the aliveness and aesthetics emerged and made up the majority of conversations (43 out of 76 quotes). The aliveness was a crucial incentive for the users to take the initiatives (29 out of 43 quotes), and the responsive behaviour made them want to interact with the object even more. They were all able to recognize the zoomorphic shape as a living object, referring to it as an animal or pet, P3 even named the ball set in front of her as "Peter" and said "Goodbye, my friend" to it when left. The high colour contrast and the texture also provoked their initiatives, as the users found the colours enjoyable and vibrant. The goose down texture reminded them of the furry animals, which triggered them to pet it. There was a positive effect on the social inclusion, as the interaction caused many conversations among the seniors. For instance, P3 who had relatively high level of language ability expressed herself more frequently than others, helping other participants interact with the zoomorphic shape, as "See, you play it like this, you can touch it". The participants enjoyed the process and showed positive emotions on several occasions when interacting with *Dynamorph*. They laughed, made jokes about the design, and expressed their feeling through words. Participants with all levels of cognitive impairment were engaged well with *Dynamorph*.

The in-depth interview with the nurse confirmed the autonomous attraction of the seniors with dementia and acknowledged that this provided the seniors with dementia meaningful activity for occupation when the nurses are unable to pay attention to the seniors. Petting the object and being amazed by its movements, colours and texture kept the seniors with dementia busy, calm and avoided the situation that they started looking for confrontation with each other or engage in negative activities. The nurse emphasized the calming and positive effect *Dynamorph* brought to the seniors as: "There are people sitting there (points to table) petting for over 40 min. So you are already giving them a form of inner peace otherwise they wouldn't sit down for that long time". The peace and harmony that was rarely present were evident when interacting with *Dynamorph*. These all confirmed the effects on users' positive affection, and further on their quality of life.

6 Conclusion and Future Work

Dynamorph was presented with the intention of providing meaningful engagement and levelled stimulations based on the conditions of senior residents with dementia in long-term care facilities. A four-layer interaction design inspired by the Montessori method was proposed. The prototype was then evaluated, using a qualitative research approach for data analysis. The result of the evaluation indicated that *Dynamorph* was able to bring calmness among users, which would lead to reduced agitation, moreover helping to form communication and positive social behaviours [24]. The calmness and harmony during the evaluation, and the balance between interaction and social inclusion also proved that layered interactions worked for the target user group.

Evaluation also brought useful insights that can provide guidance for future developments of this design and inspire similar developments. For instance, the users had difficulties building a logical link between the zoomorphic ball sets and the patterns that are filled with liquid. Therefore future improvement of the design should aim to increase the intuitiveness and establish a connection that is easier to understand than it is now. Furthermore, for the validation of the framework and the design, controlled long-term studies with more participants are needed for fully investigating the effectiveness of this design. Due to the limitation of the verbal language abilities of the seniors with dementia, further analysis should also consider analysis based on non-verbal signals such as facial expressions, gestures and movements [25].

Acknowledgments. The author would like to thank the Chinese Scholarship Council, T. Zuo from Jiangnan University, and Sylvia van Aggel, Helma Verstappel from Vitalis Berckelhof for their support on the study.

References

1. World Health Organization Fact Sheets on Dementia. http://www.who.int/mediacentre/factsheets/fs362/en/
2. Moyle, W., Venturato, L., Griffiths, S., et al.: Factors influencing quality of life for people with dementia: a qualitative perspective. Aging Ment. Health **15**(8), 970–977 (2011)
3. Cruz, J., Marques, A., Barbosa, A., et al.: Making sense(s) in dementia: a multisensory and motor-based group activity program. Am. J. Alzheimer's Dis. Other Dementias **28**(2), 137–146 (2013)
4. Draper, B.: Understanding Alzheimer's & Other Dementias. Longuevill Books, Woolahra (2011)
5. Cohen-Mansfield, J., Marx, M.S., Freedman, L.S., et al.: The comprehensive process model of engagement. Am. J. Geriatr. Psychiatry **19**(10), 859–870 (2011)
6. Livingston, G., Kelly, L., Lewis-Holmes, E., et al.: Non-pharmacological interventions for agitation in dementia: systematic review of randomised controlled trials. Br. J. Psychiatry **205**(6), 436–442 (2014)
7. Cohen-Mansfield, J., Marx, M.S., Dakheel-Ali, M., et al.: Can persons with dementia be engaged with stimuli? Am. J. Geriatr. Psychiatry **18**(4), 351–362 (2010)
8. Cohen-Mansfield, J., Dakheel-Ali, M., Marx, M.S.: Engagement in persons with dementia: the concept and its measurement. Am. J. Geriatr. Psychiatry **17**(4), 299–307 (2009)
9. Van Mierlo, L.D., Van der Roest, H.G., Meiland, F.J.M., et al.: Personalized dementia care: proven effectiveness of psychosocial interventions in subgroups. Ageing Res. Rev. **9**(2), 163–183 (2010)
10. Alm, N., Dye, R., Gowans, G., et al.: A communication support system for older people with dementia. Computer **40**(5), 35–41 (2007)
11. Gitlin, L.N., Winter, L., Earland, T.V., et al.: The tailored activity program to reduce behavioral symptoms in individuals with dementia: feasibility, acceptability, and replication potential. Gerontologist **49**(3), 428–439 (2009)
12. Cohen-Mansfield, J., Parpura-Gill, A., Golander, H.: Utilization of self-identity roles for designing interventions for persons with dementia. J. Gerontol. Psychol. Sci. **61**(4), 202–212 (2006)

13. Phinney, A., Chaudhury, H., O'connor, D.L.: Doing as much as I can do: the meaning of activity for people with dementia. Aging Ment. Health **11**(4), 384–393 (2007)
14. Kolanowski, A., Buettner, L.: Prescribing activities that engage passive residents: an innovative method. J. Gerontol. Nurs. **34**(1), 13–18 (2008)
15. Montessori, M., Gutek, G.L.: The Montessori Method: The Origins of an Educational Innovation. Rowman & Littlefield, Lanham (2004)
16. Camp, C.J.: Origins of Montessori programming for dementia. Non-pharmacol. Ther. Dement. **1**(2), 163–174 (2010)
17. Sheppard, C.L., McArthur, C., Hitzig, S.L.: A systematic review of Montessori-based activities for persons with dementia. J. Am. Med. Dir. Assoc. **17**(2), 117–122 (2016)
18. Malone, M.L., Camp, C.J.: Montessori-based dementia programming: providing tools for engagement. Dementia **6**, 150–157 (2007)
19. Orsulic-Jeras, S., Schneider, N.M., Camp, C.J., et al.: Montessori-based dementia activities in long-term care: training and implementation. Activ. Adapt. Aging **25**(3–4), 107–120 (2001)
20. Rauterberg, M., Feijs, L.: Enhanced causation for design. Int. J. Philos. Study **3**, 21–34 (2015)
21. Kahneman, D.: Maps of bounded rationality: a perspective on intuitive judgment and choice. Nobel Prize Lect. **8**, 351–401 (2002)
22. Day, K., Carreon, D., Stump, C.: The therapeutic design of environments for people with dementia: a review of the empirical research. Gerontol. Soc. Am. **40**(4), 397–416 (2000)
23. Liu, H., Hu, J., Rauterberg, M.: Follow your heart: heart rate controlled music recommendation for low stress air travel. Interact. Stud. **16**(2), 303–339 (2015)
24. Hu, J.: Social things: design research on social computing. In: Rau, P.-L.P. (ed.) CCD 2016. LNCS, vol. 9741, pp. 79–88. Springer, Cham (2016). https://doi.org/10.1007/978-3-319-40093-8_9
25. Barakova, E.I., Lourens, T.: Expressing and interpreting emotional movements in social games with robots. Pers. Ubiquitous Comput. **14**(5), 457–467 (2010)

AR Sound Sandbox: A Playful Interface for Musical and Artistic Expression

Bastian Dewitz[1], Roman Wiche[1], Chris Geiger[1],
Frank Steinicke[2], and Jochen Feitsch[1(✉)]

[1] Duesseldorf University of Applied Sciences, Duesseldorf, Germany
{bastian.dewitz,geiger,jochen.feitsch}@hs-duesseldorf.de,
roman.w92@web.de
[2] University of Hamburg, Hamburg, Germany
steinicke@informatik.uni-hamburg.de

Abstract. In this paper we introduce a novel interface combining spatial and continuous tangible interaction for creating and manipulating audio-visual effects. Our goal is to provide a ready-to-use, "hands-on" interface that does not need protracted explanation to the user, yet provides possibilities for expression. Therefore, our interface exploits the three-dimensional topology of physical sand, which is distributed over a tabletop surface. We discovered, that users of the system were engaged by the natural interaction and playful manner of the installation, as it resembles the play in a sandbox. We demonstrate an artistic setup that produces ambient soundscapes using a Lattice Boltzmann based particle simulation running through a deformable landscape. Visual feedback is front-projected onto the sand as well as the user's hand. The user can explore and change the landscape by using his or her hands and use spatial gestures via on-body projection to control AR content and further settings. The focus of this work lies on the simultaneous interaction with sand and the user's own body, and it's contribution to audio-visual installations.

Our prototype system was tested with potential users in a small informal study and was overall well received. Users had fun exploring the different forms of interaction techniques to control the particle simulation and soundscape, and were amazed by the possibilities of on-body interaction. In future we plan to further evaluate our system in a formal study and compare interaction and user experience to similar interfaces. The system was successfully deployed as an indoor room installation, reducing it's components to a minimum. Further deployments are planned.

Keywords: Musical human-computer interaction
Haptic and force feedback devices
Interactive sound art and installations
Novel controllers and interfaces for musical expression
Continuous tangible user interfaces · On-body interaction
Spatial user interface · Projection mapping

© ICST Institute for Computer Sciences, Social Informatics and Telecommunications Engineering 2018
Y. Chisik et al. (Eds.): INTETAIN 2017, LNICST 215, pp. 59–76, 2018.
https://doi.org/10.1007/978-3-319-73062-2_5

1   Introduction

Despite the advances in technologies for interacting with computer systems over the last years, operating computers is still mostly based on mouse, keyboard or recently touch screens. This form of interaction differs from the natural interaction with the real environment. Therefore, researchers have been investigating for the last decades how new forms of human computer interaction can become more similar to the interaction with the real world.

One approach to tackle this problem is investigated in the research field of tangible user interfaces (TUI). The basic idea behind TUIs is to use natural interaction with real objects in the real environment to control digital content. The mapping between physical objects and digital content is done in different ways, for example, by combining them modularly or by arranging them spatially. Objects that map physical manipulation onto digital data are called tangibles.

Especially the research area of new musical interfaces frequently yields new prototype systems for musical expression that adopt HCI-concepts for natural and tangible interaction. Some of these prototypes can be rather successful, for example reacTable, which was developed since 2003 by Jordà [6] and can now even be used as a new instrument in live performances. Interaction techniques and metaphors vary strongly between prototypes so a vast quantity of different systems exists. Qualitative user studies show promising results for new forms of collaborative interaction, user experience and entertainment [1,6,7]. However, a rarely used approach for musical interfaces are continuous tangible user interfaces, a concept of TUIs developed in 2002 by MIT media laboratory [9].

In our approach for a new way of musical expression we transfer the sculpting of a landscape to the sculpting of a soundscape. We combine tangible interaction, interactive augmented reality (AR) content and on-body interaction in our system to create a novel way of interacting with music and sound. The user can interact with the system by using only his or her hands and does not need any additional input devices. Therefore, the system is ready-to-use: once set up, users can interact with an installation without further requirements. We developed a prototype to evaluate this concept for interaction in a user study to identify possible applications and potentials. While the basic interaction of sculpting the sand is self-explanatory, the advanced interaction techniques require a short explanation.

The remainder of this paper structures as follows: First we give an overview of continuous tangible user interfaces for musical expression and on-body interaction prototypes that have been developed in the last years. Then we present design concepts and implementation details of our own approach. We proceed by presenting observations made during a qualitative user study conducted with our system. We conclude with a discussion of these observation and plans on further development and evaluation of our system.

2   Related Work

We combine two new approaches for spatial human-computer interaction in our system: continuous tangible user interfaces and on-body interaction. In the following we give an outline of continuous tangible user interfaces for musical expression and on-body interaction prototype systems.

2.1   Interfaces for Musical Expression

There are plenty examples of TUI based prototype systems for musical expression: A common approach is to utilize tangible artifacts to control certain aspects of music, for example, fading volume by turning a tangible. The spatial arrangement of these artifacts is used for interaction with music and influences the behavior of spatially close artifacts. By this, the tangibles become a metaphor of the music itself, controlling main parameters and influencing each other. Research results show that these kind of interfaces are generally well received and both easy and fun to use [1,6], in some aspects facilitate interaction, for example, concerning multi-user-interaction, and allow for a playful exploration of the interface [6]. However, there are just very few prototype systems that explore the application of continuous tangible user interfaces as interaction concept:

Granulatsynthese was an early attempt in 2008 to create a music interface using a continuous deformable surface [1]. It is highly focused on the individual user experience and not determined to enable the user to create sounds or music in a performance way. Beckhaus et al. used a granular half-transparent substance as a haptic input medium. The user would dig holes that were detected by an infrared light system. Depending on the operating preset and the created shapes the user would hear synthetic sounds and see matching computer generated sound-waves, which are projected onto to granules from the backside, resulting in a mesmerizing atmosphere [1]. Granulatsynthese was tested multiple times on different occasions and with different test subjects. Beckhaus et al. describe a playful interaction with the system and exploratory behavior. They especially point out the importance of the tangible medium as it significantly influences the haptic experience.

In 2014 the students project Sand Noise Device [11] features a sandbox as sound generating game-like device. Users can place tangible glowing pucks on a sand surface which is captured by a Kinect sensor. AR content is projected onto the sand from top. In fixed time intervals sound bursts are emitted from these pucks and a central emitter along with projected particles. These particles move through the sand landscape to the lowest point in their vicinity. The velocity of each particle is then mapped to a sound generation in MaxMSP. The system received some media attention and was overall well received but unfortunately neither further evaluated nor scientifically published.

A recent approach is soundFORMS [2], a synthesizer and sequencer created by MIT media Lab in 2016. It allows users to shape waveforms and drum-loops with a predefined set of gestures, for example, a chopping down movement with one hands to create a sawtooth waveform, which is then rendered as audio. The system uses a 24 × 24 matrix of motorized pins that change the appearance of the surface according to the created sound-waves.

2.2 On-Body Interaction Prototypes

The research field of on-body projection and interaction is a very young research area with a small number of prototypes that primarily demonstrate the feasibility of this new concept for interacting with digital content. The basic idea behind on-body interaction is to use the human body as input or output device by projecting computer generated interactive content onto specific body parts. Usually such a system consist of three components [5]: A tracking device that allows to determine the 3D-position of body parts in the real world, a projector that projects content onto these points and a computer that allows interaction with the projected content. In most cases, content is projected onto the users hands or arms as these body parts can be easily placed in field of view and provide our primary tool for interacting with the real world [5].

In the past few years, driven by the advancing technological possibilities, stationary [4,12] and wearable [3,5,8] prototypical systems have been successfully developed. Many systems rely on depth [3,4,12] or RGB [8] camera data and use computer vision algorithms to detect relevant body parts or movement. Depending on the usage scenario, different forms of interaction have been tested, in many cases some form of gestural input [4,8,12] or touch event based interaction with virtual AR buttons and sliders [3,5]. In some cases, the surrounding environment is used as an additional projection area [8,12]. Overall, despite the feasibility of the concept of on-body interaction, no best practices for technologies or interaction have been established yet.

3   Projection-Based AR Sound Sandbox

As there is no direct analogy between sculpting a sand surface and creating a soundscape, it is possible to freely design different approaches for interacting with sound. The concept in this approach was developed considering following criteria:

- Easy to understand reaction of the system to input of the user, allowing a deliberate manipulation of produced sound. The user controls the volume levels of different soundscape tracks.
- Correspondence between visual effects and audio.
- Combine AR content, on-body interaction and deformation of the sand surface to control the system.
- Create a system that is fun to interact with.

3.1   Setup

Our sandbox uses a setup similar to Piper and Ishiis Illuminating clay [9] respectively Sand Noise Device [11]. We use a 0.6 m × 0.4 m plexiglass box that is filled

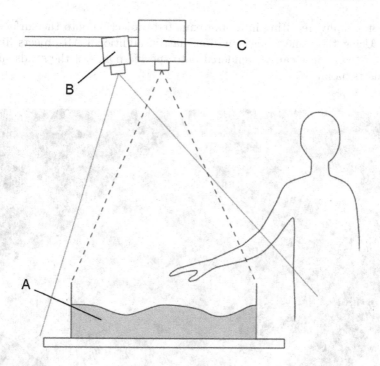

Fig. 1. Prototype setup. A: deformable sand surface, B: projector, C: depth sensor.

with 0.1 m kinetic sand. We chose kinetic sand as haptic medium because of its interesting haptic features and its easy formability into firm structures. To provide preferably genuine projection features, we used a special white-colored sand. We placed a Kinect 2 sensor and a small projector (Optoma ML750e) 1.2 m above the sand surface, both facing downwards (see Fig. 1). In this setup the Kinect 2 sensor provides a 184 × 120 pixels wide depth image of the sandbox and user hands positioned above the surface. The system we are using is a Windows 8.1 PC equipped with an Intel i7-3930k CPU, 8 GB Ram and a Geforce GTX 770. Our development environment is the game engine Unity 5.

3.2 Projection

To project AR content onto the deformable sand surface, we determine the transformation matrix between Kinect sensor space and projector image space. This allows rendering a background image onto the sand to colorize the surface in different color schemes. We use a dynamic grid that deforms accordingly to the sand's topography to correctly project a colored background image. First we define the outline of the sandbox in the Kinect depth image with the four vertices of a quad. This quad is then divided into a grid of 32 × 32 cells. Each vertex of these cells has a distinct 3D-position in Kinect space which can be transformed into 2D projector space coordinates to distort a textured mesh to match the sands topography, resulting in a approximated projection onto the surface (see Fig. 2). Using the same transformation matrix, additional AR-objects like 3D models or 2D images can be rendered onto specific points of the sands surface or the users hand.

Fig. 2. Distorted grid projected onto the sand surface

We aimed for a harmonized presentation of sound and visual effects to boost creativity during interaction. Therefore, we defined two exemplary presets called *moods*. One preset is a calm setting with nice and warm sound, together with blue and violet colors, the other a sinister setting with dark and unpleasant sound supplemented by a red and black color scheme. The sands topography is colorized according to these color schemes by mapping the height value of each pixel of the height map provided by the Kinect onto a color ramp and projecting the resulting texture onto the sand. Using different color ramps, it is possible to create diverse visual impressions of the surface (see Fig. 3).

3.3   Simulation and Sound Synthesis

To achieve natural and naive to understand interaction, we decided to use a real-time fluid simulation that moves particles from left to right through the sands topography. Up to eight virtual AR sound points are placed onto the surface by the user. Each of these points attracts nearby particles and absorbs them, if they touch it. The rate of incoming particles of every point can be mapped onto an

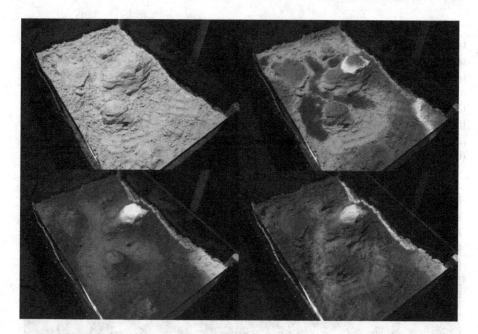

Fig. 3. Different visualization of height values using color ramps (Color figure online)

arbitrary sound parameter. In our system we chose to control the volume of pre-defined audio samples as it is an easy comprehensible way to interact with sound. To do this, the number of absorbed particles over a certain time is counted for every AR sound point, directly controlling the volume of the appropriate audio sample. We identified eight AR sound points and thus audio samples to offer an extensive amount of combination options for musical expression. The sound effects can easily be changed by replacing the audio samples (preferably using loop-able samples of a certain length). For advanced requirement we added OSC-support as a way to control other applications especially dedicated to creating music or sound via network. The decisions made focused mainly on the ease of use of the installation. The particle stream behaves in water-like manner that is easily understandable for the user.

We use a GPU-shader that simulates up to 8 million particles in real time and renders them onto a full-hd texture that is added to the background texture. To simulate real word behavior and thus predictable system reactions to user actions, we use a two dimensional Lattice Boltzmann simulation (LBM) in a multi-relaxation D2Q9-model to create water-like flows of particles (see Fig. 4). Hills and steep horizontal edges are detected in the Kinects depth image and added as obstacles in real time using an obstacle texture as shader input. LBM allows controlling the degree of turbulences by adjusting a single parameter [10] and can be implemented efficiently on the GPU. We selected a relaxation time value of $\tau = 1.98$ that creates both predictable and visual interesting flow effects. This value was selected through try-and-error.

The direction and velocity of the fluid is stored for each pixel in a fluid force texture. Additionally we create a same sized gradient map of the topography that describes the direction of the steepest slope for each point and drag particles towards this direction. Further, particles are attracted to AR-soundpoints with a gravity-like force. Each particle moving through the topography can look up the fluid and gradient force by accessing the stored pixel values at their position in 2D-space and calculate the attracting force of each soundpoint. All forces are then weighted and added in every frame to form a combined force that determines the momentary flow direction of each particle.

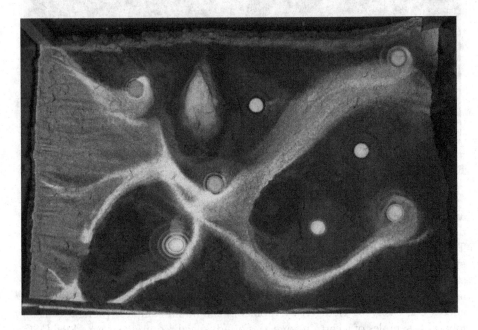

Fig. 4. Virtual particles flowing through the topography

3.4   Hand Tacking

For interacting with AR content we implemented a heuristic approach for hand tracking using depth data form the Kinect 2 sensor. We combine two different tracking methods: contour tracking and segment tracking.

Contour tracking is a popular approach to detect fingers in RBG-images. The background of a image is algorithmically removed so only pixels of the users hands are left. This can be easily performed in depth images as it is possible to remove all pixels that are farther away than a defined background threshold. The outline of the remaining pixels can be further examined to detect fingertips and other contour points of interest by their distinct features. In this project we use the radial distance method [13] to detect fingertips positions.

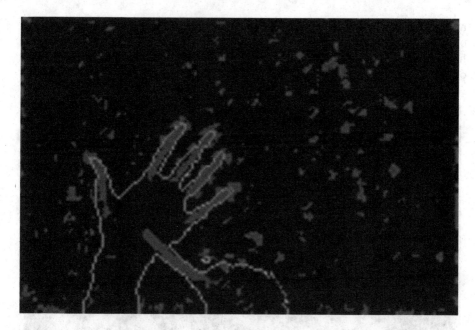

Fig. 5. Positive response (red) to fingerlike objects in the depth image (Color figure online)

During on-body interaction one hand masks the other so that contour tracking alone is not sufficient. In this case we detect finger-like objects in the image with a custom template matching algorithm that responds positive to pixels that are bounded by two opposing steep edges in vertical, horizontal or diagonal direction (see Fig. 5). A similar approach was presented in [3] for horizontal fingers. Positive responding pixels are then converted to a binary image which is segmented to identify connected positive responding pixels. If a segment's area size lies between a minimal and a maximal adjustable threshold it is considered a finger. We determine the distance between the lower positioned left hand and fingers of the right hand to detect touch events. If the distance of any finger lies below 15 mm, a value that is mostly defined by the Kinect sensors noise, a touch event is initiated at that position.

Our custom on-body hand tracking system was designed specifically for the presented setup and focused on resource efficiency to guarantee low-latency interaction and jerk-free visualization of the particle stream even on non state-of-the-art computers. It was not compared to known available hand tracking systems, as all requirements could be met.

3.5 Interaction Techniques

Interaction with the system is based on three different concepts:

First, it is possible to interact with the kinetic sand in a very natural way, like a child playing in a sand box. The user can sculpt the surface with both hands and watch the resulting changes of the particle flow. He or she can construct walls or hills that deflect the particles onto AR points or away from them. Forming holes causes particles to accumulate and digging ditches allows a precise control of particle streams.

Fig. 6. A user interacting with the menu projected onto his hand

Second, the user controls AR content and settings from the on-body menu which is projected onto the left hand if it's palm is facing upwards and it's thumb spread away (see Fig. 6). This pose is unlikely to occur during interaction, but easy to achieve deliberately, when the user wants to use the menu. To differentiate whether the system recognizes a left hand palm up or a right hand palm down, the user's position is tracked and estimated by the depth-sensor as well. For interaction we use a graphical menu projected onto the users hand controlled by touch and swipe events (see Fig. 6). Considering todays wide spread of mobile devices like smart phones and tablets, control by touch and swipe is presumably an easy to learn interaction technique for many potential users. Thus we implemented touch buttons and swipe gestures to scroll through a list of buttons as these are some of the most basic actions in mobile smart phones. Using this menu, the user can control essential features in our systems like adding new AR soundpoints onto the sand or remove existing points. Additionally, the user can switch between the two *moods* to change the produced sounds and production environment according to his or her needs.

Last, the user can perform gestural input. Depending on the operating mode, the user can delete or remove existing points. In order to do so, the user can select AR points by pointing a finger at them, just like indicating specific objects in the real world (see Fig. 7). The selection of the point is triggered after a short delay, to avoid the midas touch problem. Depending on the interaction mode, the selected point is than either removed from the sand surface or attached to the selecting finger to be placed somewhere else. The midas touch problem describes the difficulty of differentiating intended selection and thus positively provoking an event from unintended saccades that occur in human movement. Placing a AR point is handled in a similar way by pointing to the desired location. Further, the user can push particles with hand swipes in any direction or use his or her hand to temporarily block the particle flow.

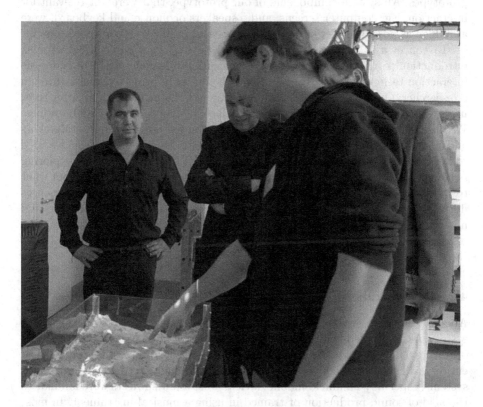

Fig. 7. Several users interacting with and watching the exhibit

4   Evaluation

We carried out an informal user study during an exhibition of the system. We observed subjects during interaction with the system to get a first impression of how our system would affect user experience and how long users, who are interacting with the system for the first time, would need to comprehend the interaction techniques. The exhibition's participants were invited and had vastly divergent backgrounds. Our artistic installation was one of several exhibits, and users could approach it freely, interact autonomously or watch non-interactively (see Fig. 7). We observed both interaction with and without support by a developer.

4.1   Material and Methods

We used the sandbox described in this paper in a slightly darkened room during an exhibition of several mixed-reality and human-computer interaction research prototypes. All system components of our prototype, that were not relevant for interaction, e.g. computer screens, audio speakers or mouse and keyboard, were as hidden as possible to let subjects focus on the sandbox and projected content.

To convey the idea behind our system, we first gave some users a quick introduction to the system and design concepts by demonstration of the basic interaction techniques with the sand and the on-body projected menu through a researcher. Other users approached the system without mediation. After that, users were allowed to freely explore the interface by themselves and ask questions. We observed users during their interaction and noted down actions, statements and emotional reactions to generate qualitative data. During observation we tried to be as neutral as possible to avoid influencing the users opinions or exploring behavior. The observation of one subject ended as soon as a subject did not want to interact with the system anymore. Our main interest were user experiences during interaction and the usability of the system as a whole. The users did not know that they were observed, as the observer stood slightly away from the installation, but where enlightened later and shortly interviewed (if content with the use of the collected data).

4.2   Participants

About 50 subjects, mostly male, roughly ranging in age from 20 to 50, tested our system. As mentioned before, the subjects were not invited solely for the purpose of testing our exhibit. Rather, they were a random set of the exhibition's visitor entirety. All subjects were used to interacting with media content and computer systems, especially handheld mobile devices. Just a few subjects were familiar to the field of sound production or trained in using a musical instrument. In most cases subjects spent up to 15 min interacting with the system.

4.3   Observations

To most users our system had an inviting character. Forming the kinetic sand with bare hands provided an interesting haptic perception that invoked a positive reaction in most users. However, a few subjects refused do dig in the sand with their hands and preferred to use small shovels. Visitors were impressed by the possibilities of real time particle interaction and had fun to play around with particles. The coherence between landscape sculpting and particle flow was easily perceived by all participants. The on-body interaction menu was similarly well received, yet less intuitively learned. During interaction, by-standing visitors enjoyed watching the user's interaction with the system or tried to simultaneously use the system. Many subjects commented positively on the combination of sounds and suitable visuals and thereby induced atmosphere.

In many cases subjects focused on performing specific interaction techniques and not on exploring the possibility of sound production. In most cases, the first interaction of users was digging holes or trenches to direct particle flow and shortly after that, forming hills and walls to prevent particles from reaching specific sound points. The basic interaction concept of controlling the particle flow by forming the kinetic sand was very easy to understand and for all test subjects successfully applicable. Eventually, after firstly redirecting the particle stream to hit or avoid a specific sound point, users deliberately used gestural input and moved sound points into particle streams or out of them and listened to the changing soundscape. Users needed a small number of successful trial and error passes to figure out how to perform the selection process of virtual sound points correctly.

However, the on-body interaction menu was more difficult to comprehend. Some users needed a detailed instruction on the positioning of their hands. In many cases users recognized the analogy to mobile hand held devices and were able to learn the intended interaction techniques within several actions. Overall, users switched rarely between tangible input and selection gestures on one side and on-body interaction on the other and preferred to use different interaction techniques successively.

The used technologies and algorithms were fast and accurate enough to allow precise real-time interaction. The actual latency of the system was not measured, but no user commented on this matter negatively. All visitors used the system in the designated way, no matter if they were instructed about the system before or not. Furthermore, users tended to employ slow movements, reducing the effects of potential latency. However, we recognized this factor quite late in the observation, so we can only assume why this behavior occurred. One reason might the rather soothing atmosphere of the produced soundscape. The soundscape in general was rated more pleasant than disturbing. In some cases, user hands which were uncommonly large or small were not tracked well. This was caused by the scale-invariance of the system. Future approaches will employ a relative detection method. In almost all cases subjects needed some time to accommodate to the slower and less accurate tracking of touch events compared to touch screens but were eventually able to utilize the on-body interaction menu.

5 Discussion

Our interface is a new approach for interacting with music and sound using a continuous tangible user interface. Like other prototypes in this field, it shows that users have fun interacting with systems of this kind. Especially interactive projection mapping installations are well known tools for audience fascination (the examples stated in Sect. 2 are non-exhaustive). In our system, we use the data obtained to control further dimensions, and add the possibility to change system and interaction parameters through on-body projection. Even though the study was performed in a rather simple way with an early iteration of the prototype, some observation were made that influenced our future work.

In the last years some prototypes for on-body interaction and just very few prototypes for continuous tangible music interfaces have been developed. Our prototype shows that both research fields can be combined to add abstract features to continuous tangible user interfaces and can be implemented in an ready-to-used installation. Users need just a few successful actions to learn how to use tangible interfaces and just a few minutes to transfer interaction techniques from mobile device interaction to touch-event-based on-body interaction. Combining both seems like a good approach for system design, providing a vast multiplier to the interaction options, and should be further investigated by developing new systems and evaluating them in real world scenarios to identify possibilities and applications.

Fig. 8. Interactive indoor room-sized installation, augmenting the entrance area of the tanzhaus NRW

We made observations similar to Beckhaus et al. in [1]. Users are very interested in new forms of interacting with computer systems and show a natural curiosity about exploring new ways of interacting with digital content. By using well-known objects, for example a simple sand box, and adding further digital features, new systems emerge, that provide an inviting character to users. However, most prototype systems in this area only show feasibility and introduce possible applications; a formal study on user experience and system usability that confirms these statements in a quantitative way has not been conducted yet. Using statistical data, it would be possible to compare these new approaches of human-computer interaction to more established forms of interaction.

Our interface was mainly used in a laboratory for human computer interaction, and was not exposed to a real world scenario. Possible applications can be professional sound production, therapy and entertainment. To investigate these potentials our system can be further examined with both professional and non-professional users. From a production perspective, it would be very interesting to investigate how TUI-based music interface interaction compares to the common use of synthesizers in music production and if interface-dependent effects on the creativity of an artist are measurable.

6 Deployment

The system's engine was reused in a somewhat different yet still audio-visual installation, proving the feasibility of our basic concepts. The provided task was to create an interactive indoor room-sized installation, augmenting the entrance area of the tanzhaus NRW facility. The name of the installation was "Kinetic Stream" (see Fig. 8).

We decided to reduce the interaction dimensions of the presented system to solely the well perceived particle flow simulation including terrain detection for guidance of the particle stream. This decision was made after extracting the insight from our evaluation that this part of the system was easily understandable even without any explanation. Instead of sand, the visitors themselves were detected as "landscape" in a 4 m × 4 m wide area. Additionally, the particle stream was extended to flow down the wall first, like a waterfall. In this iteration of the system, the wall did not react to user interaction.

Representing obstacles for the system, visitors to the installation could block the particle stream by standing inside the tracking area or even lie on the floor. As there were no sound points present at this versions, the amount of persons inside the tracking area was counted. Next, each person was simulated as a sound point fully loaded by particles, regardless of the visitor's actual position in the stream (resulting in triggering the playback of an additional audio sample for each user in the tracking area). As visitors were to block the particle stream as if being elevated areas in the sand box, a coincident representation as particle absorbing sound points would have been contradictory. Furthermore, users quickly understood that they could change the soundscape simply by changing the number of persons inside the tracking area.

This variation of our system was very well perceived. The amount of positive feedback encouraged further development of this reduced version of our prior suggested installation, but only for larger scale installations. Therefore, in the latest iteration, we included the radar scanner radarTOUCH[1] to include touch-detection for the particle stream on the wall. Touching the wall simulates an

---

[1] http://www.lang-ag.com/de/produkte/touch-solutions/radartouch.html.

elevated area, deflecting the particle flow. The design of the particle flow was changed to resemble water, simulating a waterfall and small river (see Fig. 9). Inside the river, a small school of fish follows the user (for further entertainment). This extended version was exhibited during another exhibition at our lab, just like the one described in "Evaluation".

Fig. 9. A user deflects the water like particle stream by standing in the tracking area

We scraped the idea of implementing the on-hand interaction in this installation, despite the opportunities this would have featured. This is mostly due to the fact that we assumed inaccuracy for the hand detection, due to the necessary distance of the depth sensor to cover a 4 m × 4 m area and due to masking effects.

Even though this reduced version will be further developed and deployed, we still want to pose the question, if the originally intended combination of spatial and continuous tangible interaction with on-body projection and interaction can provide a method of interaction that is ready-to-go and easy to learn, yet offers a vast variety of interaction options.

7 Conclusion and Future Work

Our prototype system was successfully tested. Design concepts were well received and interaction techniques were easy to comprehend. The AR-sound sandbox and the underlying concept of real-time particle interaction is a new way for creating music and sound that can presumably be improved to be usable in real life situations. In our system, the user modified the volume of predefined audio samples, but trough mapping lots of different sound generators can be addressed (see Sect. 3.3). A reduced version of our system was deployed and successfully operated for several successive days, substantiating this presumption. In this version of our system, the users engaged more with the visuals, while audio was used to create an appropriate atmosphere.

Additionally, our project and evaluation shows that stationary on-body interaction systems can be used to add further control mechanics to sometimes restricted tangible interface interaction. However, in contrast to well designed tangible interaction that utilizes much more natural forms of interaction, users need to learn how to use graphical menus that are controlled by on-body interaction. In this context, touch event based interaction seems to be a good approach, as many users are familiar to smart phones and tablets today, which allows them to transfer interaction techniques from these devices to on-body interaction.

In future approaches we want to improve our algorithms to allow for quantitative evaluation using standardized measurements for user experience e.g. User Experience Questionnaire. The conducted study does not cover long-term use of our system and the setup was not ideal for quantitative evaluating, thus, important aspects for interaction were not investigated sufficiently yet. We further want to develop comparable interfaces that adopt the interaction techniques and investigate differences during user interaction with the systems. We currently plan to create a full TUI version that uses tangible artifacts instead of AR-soundpoints, and a digital version that is controlled in a more common way of human-computer interaction via mouse and keyboard to investigate differences in usability and interaction aesthetics of these approaches.

Acknowledgments. This work was partially supported by the Creative Europe EU Program (project The Peoples Smart Sculpture).

References

1. Beckhaus, S., Schroeder-Kroll, R., Berghoff, M.: Back to the sandbox-playful interaction with granules landscapes (2008)
2. Colter, A., Davivongsa, P., Haddad, D.D., Moore, H., Tice, B., Ishii, H.: Sound-FORMS: manipulating sound through touch. In: CHI Extended Abstracts, pp. 2425–2430 (2016)
3. Harrison, C., Benko, H., Wilson, A.D.: OmniTouch: wearable multitouch interaction everywhere. In: Proceedings of the 24th Annual ACM Symposium on User Interface Software and Technology, pp. 441–450. ACM (2011)
4. Harrison, C., Ramamurthy, S., Hudson, S.E.: On-body interaction: armed and dangerous. In: Proceedings of the Sixth International Conference on Tangible, Embedded and Embodied Interaction, pp. 69–76. ACM (2012)
5. Harrison, C., Tan, D., Morris, D.: Skinput: appropriating the body as an input surface. In: Proceedings of the SIGCHI Conference on Human Factors in Computing Systems, pp. 453–462. ACM (2010)

6. Jordà, S.: Sonigraphical instruments: from FMOL to the reacTable. In: Proceedings of the 2003 Conference on New Interfaces for Musical Expression, pp. 70–76 (2003)
7. Levin, G.: The table is the score: an augmented-reality interface for real-time, tangible, spectrographic performance. In: Proceedings of the International Computer Music Conference (ICMC 2006), New Orleans, USA (2006)
8. Mistry, P., Maes, P.: SixthSense: a wearable gestural interface. In: ACM SIGGRAPH ASIA 2009 Sketches, p. 11. ACM (2009)
9. Piper, B., Ratti, C., Ishii, H.: Illuminating clay: a 3-D tangible interface for landscape analysis. In: Proceedings of the SIGCHI Conference on Human Factors in Computing Systems, pp. 355–362 (2002)
10. Razzaghian, M., Pourtousi, M., Darus, A.N.: Simulation of flow in lid driven cavity by MRT and SRT. In: Thailand: International Conference on Mechanical and Robotics Engineering (2012)
11. The Green Cat Collective: Sand Noise Device An Augmented Reality Musical Sandbox. http://www.sandnoisedevice.com/
12. Wilson, A.D., Benko, H.: Combining multiple depth cameras and projectors for interactions on, above and between surfaces. In: Proceedings of the 23nd Annual ACM Symposium on User Interface Software and Technology, pp. 273–282. ACM (2010)
13. Yoruk, E., Konukoglu, E., Sankur, B., Darbon, J.: Shape-based hand recognition. IEEE Trans. Image Process. **15**(7), 1803–1815 (2006)

Kessel Run - A Cooperative Multiplayer SSVEP BCI Game

Inês Cruz[1], Carlos Moreira[1], Mannes Poel[2(✉)],
Hugo Ferreira[1], and Anton Nijholt[2]

[1] Institute of Biophysics and Biomedical Engineering, Lisbon, Portugal
ines.cruz@campus.ul.pt
[2] Human-Media Interaction, University of Twente, Enschede, The Netherlands
m.poel@utwente.nl

Abstract. Digital game research has been rapidly growing with studies dedicated to game experience and adopting new technologies. Alongside, research in Brain-Computer Interfaces (BCI) is growing in game applications. Besides technical shortcomings, BCI research in gaming can also be lacking due to challenges such as poorly designed games that do not provide a fun experience to its players.

In this paper we present a novel multiplayer Steady-State Visually Evoked Potential (SSVEP) game - *Kessel Run* - with BCI-focused cooperative mechanics, drawing attention to the impact of game design in the user experience.

Twelve participants played Kessel Run using a 2-electrode cap and rated their experience in a questionnaire. The SSVEP performance was lower than expected, with an average classification accuracy of 55% and maximum of 79% at a 33% chance level. Despite low performances, players still reported a state of Flow, felt behaviorally involved and empathized with each other, finding it enjoyable to play the game together.

Keywords: Multi-Brain Brain-Computer Interfaces · Games
Steady-State Visually Evoked Potentials

1 Introduction

Initially, Brain-Computer Interfaces' (BCIs) primary goal was to restore communication for the physically challenged. Applications include moving a wheelchair [1], spelling through a device [2], among others. However BCI devices are progressively becoming smaller and more affordable. Easy-to-use Electroencephalography (EEG)-based BCI headsets such as the Emotiv EPOC or the NeuroSky®'s MindWave have appeared in the market, leading to their usage outside the medical field and towards healthy user industries, like entertainment. In particular, the gaming industry is embracing BCI as an acceptable interaction modality given its potential to enhance user experience by offering something that current interaction modalities do not [3].

© ICST Institute for Computer Sciences, Social Informatics and Telecommunications Engineering 2018
Y. Chisik et al. (Eds.): INTETAIN 2017, LNICST 215, pp. 77–95, 2018.
https://doi.org/10.1007/978-3-319-73062-2_6

Among the BCIs implemented for games, the first trend was to adapt previously made games conceived for traditional inputs. Classic games like Pacman [4], Pinball [5] or Tetris [6] were successfully used to demonstrate the application of BCIs in gaming. The rest are original, newly-developed games but these are usually proofs of concept and often do not take into account proper game design, an important requirement for every user that intends to play. Because BCI depends so much on what control paradigm is used, the interaction may vary and game developers must understand the characteristics of a specific BCI in order to design game mechanics that take advantage of its interaction. Multiplayer games, even though extremely popular in the gaming community [7], are not a very common genre in BCI games with only a few examples existing [8–11].

Gürkök et al. tried to build a BCI game framework from their research experiences in both the BCI and games communities [12]. They mentioned that "challenge", "fantasy" and "sociality" made a difference in BCI games, increasing users' motivation to play, and briefly described the ways BCI games can satisfy each of these motivations. Controlling a BCI can be challenging by itself, as it is an imperfect recognition technology. It requires players to show continuous effort and even repeat their actions until they are understood by the BCI. Nevertheless, a game should offer challenges that match the player skills in order to provide Flow [13]. Games also let players do things that they usually cannot do in real life. In a virtual world, the feeling of presence can be achieved by having a good correspondence of player actions to in-game actions. Some people enjoy playing computer games not necessarily for the challenge or the fantasy but just to be with others. Spending time with friends and seeing their reactions and expressions are huge motivations to play games socially [13]. Any multiplayer BCI game can also provide such an interactive environment. Players may cooperate or compete using BCI and they can share their experiences, such as difficulties or enjoyment with control, while playing the game.

Our game, Kessel Run is introduced as a multiplayer BCI game to breach the gap between fun games and BCI games. There is a need to create original BCI games that follow good game design practices and introduce mechanics that best suit the control paradigm. A large amount of developers consider "ease of playing the game" and "exciting application" as some of the most important elements of games [3]. Our goal was to create a BCI game that could be played outside the laboratory, with a short training period and that was as exciting as a non-BCI game. Since multiplayer games are a popular genre among gamers and sociality is one of the largest motivations to play, we chose to develop a 2-player game that can be played socially with a friend.

This paper is divided in the following sections: Sect. 2 introduces the BCI game developed and its mechanics according to a set of derived game design rules. Section 3 explains the experimental set-up, procedure and data analysis carried out, leading to Sect. 4 in which the players' performance and user experience is discussed. Finally we present our conclusions for this study in Sect. 5.

2   Kessel Run

In this section we will explore the methodologies used in the design, development and implementation of our BCI game. We start by introducing the good game design rules that were implemented throughout our game, before briefly introducing the game itself - *Kessel Run* -, its goals and simplified gameplay. After, we give an explanation on Kessel Run's BCI-focused multiplayer mechanics and the different game elements introduced, along with some considerations about our BCI paradigm selection. Finally, we approach the technical side of Kessel Run's implementation, going over our software choices and their integration.

2.1   Game Design Requirements

In this study our goal is to design a BCI-specific game that is able to provide a fun experience for its players. In order to achieve this, we derived a set of rules and concepts from good design theories applied in BCI games, mostly from Csikszentmihalyi's Flow theory [14] and Salen & Zimmerman's Paradox of Control [15]. While the Flow theory describes the immersion in a game as a state in which the player is actively engaged and where his skills match the challenge level of the game (the Flow Zone), the Paradox of Control assumes that in a state of Flow the player must feel in control of the events, while at the same time feeling the possibility of losing control due to his own failure. Together, these essentially state that in order to achieve Flow the player has to feel both in control of his skills and challenged by the game.

Based on the Flow components noted by [14] and summarized by [16], we formulated a set of requirements that must be fulfilled in order to achieve a good game design:

- The game must feature a clear goal.
- The game must have clear rules.
- The game must challenge the players' skills.
- The game should be controlled by the BCI paradigm.

In addition, it is also necessary to take into consideration the fact that Kessel Run is a cooperative multiplayer game. Several attempts have been made to identify the building blocks and the essential components of collaborative games. Wendel et al. [17] have combined and augmented previous guidelines with the purpose to stimulate the development of social skills such as team-work, communication, and coordination during game play. Some of the most important components that can be used in the design of cooperative games are a common goal/success, collaborative tasks, inter-dependent roles among players and communication.

Based on the components identified by [17], we add the list of requirements to achieve the desired interaction between players in a cooperative game:

- The players must have a common success.
- The game must feature collaborative tasks.
- The players should have inter-dependent roles.
- The game should allow for communication between the players.

2.2   Kessel Run

Kessel Run is the computer game developed for our experimental purposes. Built on the cross-platform game engine Unity $5^{®1}$, the game world contains a moving spaceship navigating through an asteroid field (Fig. 1). Being a 2-person multiplayer game, the players' goal is to survive a 2 min space race by cooperating with one another, losing only the smallest possible amount of fuel in the process. The steering of the spaceship is shared by both players (each player controls one of the propellants' movement), and therefore cooperation is needed in order to win the game. To win the game, the spaceship needs to last the entire 2 min race without losing all fuel, which decreases every time the ship is hit by an asteroid. The game is lost if fuel is zero before the race ends.

(a) Start game with a connection warning   (b) Gameplay

Fig. 1. Screengrabs from the Kessel Run computer game.

2.3   Game Mechanics

In Kessel Run we looked into building a game that is designed specifically for BCI control and can also provide an exciting experience for its players. Guided by the requirements introduced in Sect. 2.1, in Kessel Run we applied a set of elements, rules, and interesting mechanics that we will now describe.

Elements. To keep Kessel Run interesting for its players, it is necessary to include elements that make it not only enjoyable, but also that aid in deriving meaning from the game's sets of rules and goals. The elements described can be seen in Fig. 2.

The **Asteroids** can be found floating around space and are meant to satisfy the need for challenge in the players' skill, since these damage the spaceship and reduce fuel. Asteroids are spawned at random locations around the player's perimeter at every frame of the game, and have different sizes and rotations.

The **Fuel Power Ups** are scattered randomly around space, but are more scarce and much smaller than asteroids. By gathering fuel power ups the players

---

[1] Unity $5^{®}$, from Unity Technologies - https://unity3d.com.

are able to keep their fuel level high and therefore win the race. However, because these are small and rare, gathering them is not trivial.

Besides these in-game elements, several on-screen components were added to Kessel Run. The **Fuel Bar** indicates the amount of fuel left on the spaceship, while the **Timer** shows how much time is left until the race ends and the players win. There is also the players' **Control Panel**, which displays two arrows that turn red when the player moves in that respective direction. As we will explain later, the players must cooperate in order to steer the spaceship properly and therefore the Control Panel helps them visually understand the other player's movement, while also keeping both aware of their options in terms of spaceship movement.

In a more practical perspective, the **Connectivity Indicator** is always present for each player under his Control Panel and indicates whether or not the BCI software is acquiring data and connected to the game. This provides a sanity check and prevents any experimental mistakes. The indicator is orange when the system is not connected, and turns green when it is fully operational.

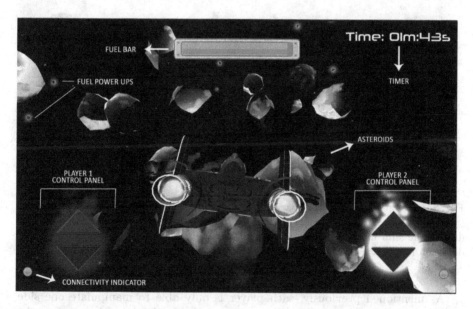

Fig. 2. Kessel Run - multiplayer BCI game in which players must cooperate with each other to navigate through an asteroid field. Several on-screen elements indicate players' status such as time left to win the game, fuel level, and an indicator of software connectivity.

Lastly, we also introduced the possibility for one player to take control of the entire spaceship by himself ('*Take Over*' command). Players can only take over when a red button periodically appears at the screen bottom, and the first player to press it takes over the spaceship for a total of 5 s. When one player takes over he is able to control the spaceship alone, although being restricted to only going up or down, making the second player unnecessary for playing the game. This functionality is intended to stimulate players' competitive behavior and was introduced as a way to offer choices in the gameplay.

Rules. The game must be governed by a set of rules which the players make use to achieve their goal and win the game. In Kessel Run, these rules are translated into the restricted movement of the spaceship and on the fuel points system, as well as the timer of the race itself.

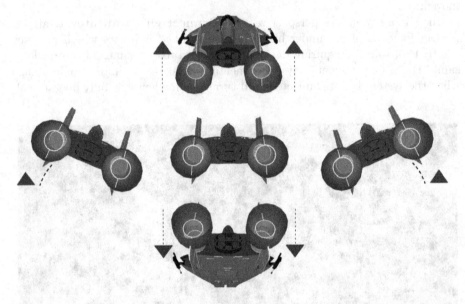

Fig. 3. Game mechanics in the spaceship movement. Each player controls the direction (up or down) of one propellant. If both players move their respective propellers up (or down), the ship moves in that direction. Otherwise, the wing rotates in the selected direction (e.g. left propellant rotates to the right when player goes up).

As mentioned previously, each player is only able to manipulate one side of the spaceship. As a result both have to work together in order to steer the ship in the desired direction. Since each player controls their respective ship's propellant, they each have only two possible movements: up or down. We chose to restrict this motion for two reasons; while being restrained would force the players to work together and create a more fun game, it also reduces the degrees of freedom for the BCI. Because each player only has three choices (steer up, down, or stay in the same place), this simplifies the classification process which we will introduce later on.

Although the players are individually restricted, together they can combine the two movements to steer the spaceship in different directions (see Fig. 3).

Since each player only controls one propellant, if he chooses to move alone the spaceship will be tilted in its respective side. Otherwise, if both chose to go in the same direction they can move the entire ship, or tilt at a higher degree when going on opposite directions. This allows for a higher range of motion and permits space scouting for fuel power ups and the dodging of asteroids.

A point system is a frequent rule implemented in several games. Here, points are disguised as fuel. The race starts with 100% fuel, and every time the ship is hit by an asteroid (by not dodging efficiently) fuel decreases by 5% of the initial value. The only chance players have of regaining fuel is by passing a Fuel Power Up, which increases fuel by another 5%. If the ship reaches 0% fuel at any given time, then the game is over and the players lose. On the other hand, if players manage to keep fuel above 0% until the 2-min timer ends, then the race is won.

In Kessel Run, as in many games, the points system serves two purposes: while they clarify the game's goal (number of points must be above zero to win), they also provide further challenge in the game; players can chose whether they simply want to beat the game, or improve their score. Providing these types of choices in the game helps keeping the players in the Flow Zone since the difficulty can be adjusted to the player's needs.

2.4   Paradigm Selection

When dealing with BCI games, the paradigm selection must be carefully considered. Some paradigms might prove more useful for BCI gaming than others. Paradigms may be more accurate, have a higher sense of control, or simply offer higher speed or more dimensions of control. Furthermore, all paradigms will have their own potential as well as limitations with respect to the paradox of control. This leaves us with the task of selecting the best paradigm for achieving an occurrence of the paradox of control.

Among the three types of paradigms (active, passive and reactive [3]), we opted to use a reactive paradigm because these have relative low illiteracy rate (89% of the users are able to get an 80% accuracy or higher after only a short training [18]) and can be used without requiring long training sessions. Moreover, using the Steady-State Visually Evoked Potentials (SSVEP) paradigm in Kessel Run provides a continuous control since the BCI detects user's intention for as long as he attends the stimuli (flickering lights). The SSVEPs requires little to no training, have low illiteracy rates [19] and more importantly, when placing external LEDs for SSVEP stimulus the space on the computer screen is no longer occupied with BCI and is free to be solely dedicated to the game. Before proceeding it is important to note that SSVEP also has downsides. Having the player concentrate on stimuli constantly can become very tiresome and uncomfortable to the player [12], particularly for the SSVEP paradigm as it features a constant flickering and could potentially break immersion in the game [20]. We attempt to counteract these downsides by making each game last a relatively small amount of time.

After selecting our paradigm, we must implement it as a game controller. For our game two red solid LED lights are placed on the top and bottom's midline of each player's screen for the up and down directions, respectively. Using external LEDs as visual stimuli avoids the limited number of frequencies of use due to monitor's refresh rate. The flickering is done at 15 and 12 Hz, detected on the 10–20 system's Pz or/and Oz electrodes, and using Canonical Correlation Analysis (CCA) as a detection method [21].

The CCA algorithm is implemented in MATLAB® and used in real-time during the game. The algorithm uses blocks of 80 samples for each iteration on acquired data. Since the sampling frequency is 512 Hz for our system, a player's decision is made every 0.15 s, offering a very smooth control.

Before each play session, the player's algorithm settings are defined empirically by selecting which electrode combination (Pz and/or Oz) and CCA threshold offers a better performance.

2.5 Software Integration

We now review the technical implementation of our multiplayer game. In the previous sections we have mentioned already two of the core softwares used to build our system: Unity 5® and MATLAB®.

After developing the game in Unity and implementing the BCI paradigm in MATLAB, we are left with two pieces of software that are not specifically designed to interact with each other. Furthermore, MATLAB is scarcely used as a real-time processing tool due to being slower than compiled code [22], and does not have a library to acquire data from the BCI device used.

Because of its flexibility and ease of integration with other software, we chose BCI2000®[2] for acquiring EEG data, connecting to Unity and MATLAB at the same time (and interacting with its different scripting languages), and controlling the crucial aspects of the experiment (e.g. start of acquisition, data markers and saving).

One BCI2000 session only acquires signals from one BCI system at a time; this means that for a multiplayer game such as Kessel Run, we are in need of at least 2 computers. In our set-up, we chose to have 3: the 2 players have dedicated computers that are in charge of acquiring, processing, and sending their signals to a separate PC where the game is running (Fig. 4). The communication between the player's and the game's computers was done via UDP (*User Datagram Protocol*). In our experiment, the UDP messages being sent from BCI2000 are related to the player's decision in the game: go up, down, or stay in the same position. Unity sends messages back to BCI2000 regarding the game status: beginning and end of game, and whether it was lost or won, which are then marked on the saved data.

There are two advantages of using BCI2000. First is the possibility to integrate different software components and orchestrate the data acquiring and processing. Secondly, because BCI2000 is a modular program, it is very easy to switch between BCI devices for data acquisition without the need to adapt the remaining game system. While in the present work we report using Biosemi

---

[2] BCI2000®, from Schalk Lab - http://bci2000.org/.

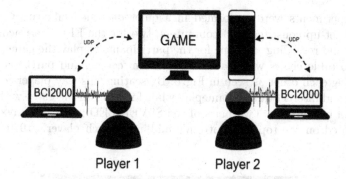

Fig. 4. UDP connection scheme: each player's computer processes the incoming brain signals, translates them into game actions, and sends them to the dedicated computer game. The computer game returns game information for marking the saved data.

ActiveTwo system for EEG data acquisition, we have tested Kessel Run with portable devices such as the Emotiv EPOC with success.

3   Methods and Materials

We invited participants to play Kessel Run in order to test if our BCI multiplayer game is capable of creating an enjoyable user experience for its players and if the SSVEP paradigm is a reliable way to control it.

3.1   Participants

All participants that volunteered to take part in this experiment were university students. We asked all participants to bring a friend, and if no friend was available they were teamed up with another participant. Participants were 12 subjects (5 female) aged 22 to 31 years old (mean age = 23.8 years old) that participated in pairs for a total of 6 game sessions. All participants reported daily computer usage. Half of the participants had no earlier experience with BCI at all, while the other half had interacted with a BCI at least once. All subjects read and signed an Informed Consent Form, verified and approved by the Ethics Committee. No subjects suffered from any neurological, psychiatric or other relevant diseases unadvised to the participation in the experiment.

3.2   Materials

EEG signals were acquired using a Biosemi ActiveTwo system[3] on a dedicated recording PC for each participant. All signals were acquired at a 512 Hz sampling rate, and two active Ag-AgCl electrodes for EEG (Pz and Oz) were placed according to the international 10–20 system.

---

[3] Biosemi ActiveTwo - http://www.biosemi.com.

The experiments were performed in a quiet darkened laboratory environment. The set-up consisted of 3 computers: two for the EEG data acquisition, processing and recording, and one for the participants to play the game. A table with comfortable chairs was placed in the room center, and participants were seated facing each other as seen in Fig. 5. By seating this way players could see each other and interact during gameplay while focusing on the game without too strong head movements. Two pairs of red SSVEP LED lights (10 cm × 10 cm) were mounted on the top and bottom's midline of each player's 1920 × 1080, 60 Hz monitor.

Fig. 5. Two participants shortly after beginning playing Kessel Run. (Color figure online)

3.3 Procedure

Before playing the game, every participant filled in a demographic questionnaire that also inquired about their gaming habits and previous BCI usage. After being explained the content of the experiment, the EEG caps and electrodes were placed on each participant. A good connectivity was ensured by applying electrolyte gel until all electrode offsets were lower than ± 20 mV. A short SSVEP session of 80 s was recorded for offline performance analysis and participant's CCA parameter definition (threshold and EEG channels used). In this session, participants were asked to look at the top and bottom LED light, and at the center of the screen every 5 s, while their EEG data was acquired using BioSemi's software, ActiView.

Participants were given time to learn the game before playing eight rounds of Kessel Run. After they played the game, every participant filled questionnaires on Game Experience and Social Presence adapted from the Game Experience Questionnaire developed by IJsselsteijn et al. [23,24]. The first module assesses game experience as scores on six components: Challenge, Competence, Flow, Tension/Annoyance, Positive and Negative Affect. The social presence module investigates psychological and behavioral involvement of the player with other social entities, in this case the co-located person playing the game with them [24]. This module consists of three components: Behavioral Involvement, Psychological Involvement - Empathy and Psychological Involvement - Negative Feelings. An extra item was added to the social presence module to assess players' intentions to cooperate with one another: 'I felt inclined to work together with the other'. For both questionnaires the items were presented on a scale of agreement from 0 to 4, in which 0 - 'not at all', 1 - 'slightly', 2 - 'moderately', 3 - 'fairly' and 4 - 'extremely'.

3.4 Data Analysis

All data was analyzed under MATLAB® and R software environment for statistical computing.

Participants' SSVEP performance was evaluated using the training session recorded during the experiment. Raw EEG signals from the back of the head (Pz and Oz) were selected and trials of 80 samples were extracted for the three conditions: looking at 12 Hz (bottom) light source, at 15 Hz (top) light source, and at the center of the computer screen. Each trial was then subject to CCA with sine and cosine reference signals at 12 and 15 Hz. Upon visual inspection the best electrode(s) and an empirical correlation threshold were set for each participant, and classification for each condition followed. No preprocessing was performed in order to minimize real-time computing costs. The resulting trials were classified into game actions according to the maximum of CCA's correlations. If the highest correlation (of the two possible values for each frequency) exceeds the participant's threshold, the decision is set to the corresponding frequency - 12 or 15 Hz -, meaning that the player goes either up or down. If the threshold isn't met, the decision to stay in the center is chosen.

For Kessel Run's game experience, each item's scores were grouped according to their respective user experience components: Challenge, Competence, Flow, Tension/Annoyance, Positive and Negative Affect. For the Social Presence questionnaire, items were grouped in three components: Behavioral Involvement, Psychological Involvement - Empathy and Psychological Involvement - Negative Feelings. After grouping, mean and standard deviation were derived from participant scores for both modules. For the single item *'I felt inclined to work together with the other'* only the frequency of responses and mean score were determined.

4 Results

We now present the results obtained from the experiment described in the previous section, in which participant pairs were asked to play our BCI game - Kessel

Run - and rate it according to its game and social experience. Along with our findings, we derive some comments and discuss the meaning for each result.

4.1 Performance

Of the initial 12 participants, two (one pair) were excluded only from performance analysis due to changes in the experimental setup.

Table 1. SSVEP performance descriptives from CCA classification (33% chance level).

	$\bar{X}(\sigma)$	Max	Min
Overall	55.3 (14.1)	78.9	34.1
12 Hz	62.7 (12.6)	85.6	47.8
15 Hz	37.8 (19.5)	80.0	20.0

Generally speaking, SSVEP performance was lower than expected. Overall classification (i.e. the 3 class decision between choosing the 12 or 15 Hz stimuli, or choosing not to move by looking at the PC's center) was 55% on average, reaching a maximum 79% (Table 1). Most participants obtained a performance above 50% (see Fig. 6), although a few remain under the it. We identified two key factors that influence these low performance values: darkness of the room, and participant detection of the used frequencies.

In order to obtain a good quality SSVEP it is necessary to isolate its visual stimuli from other light sources, usually done by darkening the experimental room to reinforce stimuli brightness. Although all of our experiments were performed under a darkened laboratory, ambient light was still present due to window gaps (visible in Fig. 5) which caused a reduction in LED brightness and consequent loss in performance.

On the other hand, a good quality SSVEP relies also on the brain's capacity to react to repetitive flickering at a certain frequency. From Fig. 6 we can note that subject's performance for the 12 Hz frequency (light blue bars) is consistently higher than at 15 Hz (yellow bars) and that its maximum (86%) and mean (63%) performance are also the highest of the three classes, meaning that participants could more easily produce SSVEPs when focusing on the 12 Hz light source but had difficulty recognizing the 15 Hz source, dragging the overall performance down. This difference in performance is likely due to the fact that the 12 Hz frequency is within the dominant alpha range. Because the 15 Hz source was generally harder to classify, the overall BCI performance is lowered and participants could either control both or only one of the spaceship's directions. Hakvoort et al. [25] too found that subject's precision in a CCA-based detection method differs according to frequencies used. Similar results were also found in [26].

Moreover one can expect that during game play the detection performance is even lower because the BCI and the game both use the visual channel. The

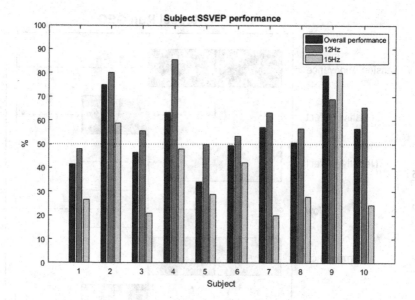

Fig. 6. SSVEP performance per subject. Light blue and yellow bars correspond to the percentage of trials correctly classified as looking at 12 and 15 Hz, respectively. Dark blue bars indicate the CCA's overall performance classifying if the subject is looking at the 12, 15 Hz light source, or not looking. (Color figure online)

different SSVEPs are induced by flickering lights above and below the screen. In order to issue a BCI command the player has to visually focus on the corresponding flickering light instead of the game. But due to the fast dynamics of the game the player also needs to focus on the video game. This results in a rapid switching of focus and no time for the SSVEP to reach a steady state in the EEG signal.

Although there might have been some misjudgment on our behalf on the SSVEP frequency selection, we observed that despite low BCI performance the players were able to adapt their game strategy, placing their head in different positions for better SSVEP detection (closer to the LED light, for example) or focusing on using only one of the controls (usually the 12 Hz) to play the game. Their adaptation could result in a feeling of higher control than what is anticipated by their classification performance, which is based solely on the recorded training session, and cause a reduced impact on the user experience.

4.2   Game Experience

To evaluate Kessel Run's user experience as a digital game we grouped responses from the Game Experience questionnaire (GEQ) into key components and results are summarized in Fig. 7.

Most likely due to low BCI performance, participants only felt slightly competent ($\overline{competence} = 1.1$) to play the game. Interestingly enough, we observed

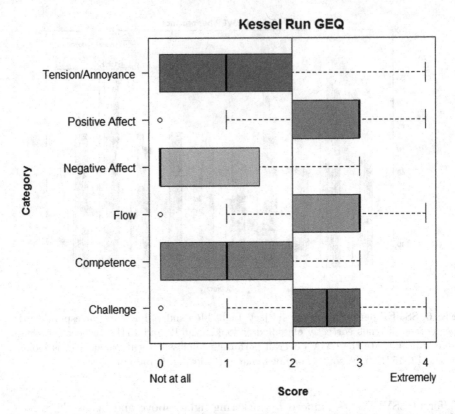

Fig. 7. Boxplot for the answers on the Game Experience questionnaire, for each of the six components: Challenge, Competence, Flow, Tension/Annoyance, Positive and Negative Affect.

that participants were able to adapt while playing Kessel Run even when not in full control of the BCI, as mentioned in the previous section. Teams often opted to move the spaceship in only one of their controllable directions in order to play together. Otherwise when one player had a better BCI performance, the other would be elected "captain" and would order directions for the spaceship to move next. These strategies helped create a greater bond between players and lead to a predominantly positive affect during the game ($\overline{pos.\,affect} = 2.5/\overline{neg.\,affect} = 0.8$). Moreover, they also lead to greater feel of immersion ($\overline{Flow} = 2.6$) during the game and a moderate to fair sense of challenge ($\overline{challenge} = 2.3$). When considering the questionnaires scores we can conclude that Kessel Run is an overall enjoyable game, specially when taking into account the participant's Flow scores, suggesting a good employment of the good design requirements appointed previously.

There is, of course, room for improvement in Kessel Run's enjoyment and the BCI paradigm selection seems to play an important role in the game's playability due to its Competence scores. It would be advantageous to substitute SSVEP with another equally or more intuitive paradigm such as motor imagery, because this paradigm is based on induced activations and not on evoked responses could provide a more intuitive and fun experience.

4.3 Social Presence

The summary of the Social Presence questionnaire (SPQ) results aggregated by component is shown in Fig. 8.

For the Behavioral Involvement component, all items had positive scores (mean above 2). This component included six items with mean scores ranging from 2.4 to 3.1 ($\overline{b.involvement}$ = 2.7). This component measures the degree to which players feel their actions to be dependent on their co-players actions. Results suggest that players considered their actions fairly dependent on the other's actions, e.g. mean (*'What the other did affected what I did'*) = 2.8.

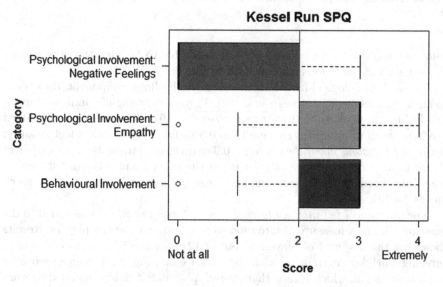

Fig. 8. Boxplot for the answers on the Social Presence questionnaire, for each of the three components: Behavioral Involvement, Psychological Involvement - Empathy and Psychological Involvement - Negative Feelings.

In the Psychological Involvement - Empathy component, all but one items had a mean score over 2 ($\overline{empathy}$ = 2.3). Of all the six items included in this component, *'I admired the other'* was the only one with a negative mean score (mean = 1.0 'slightly'). This may be due to the fact that players only felt slightly competent playing the game and didn't feel their co-players to be much more competent controlling the BCI. The remaining five items had mean scores ranging from 2.3 to 2.8. Players empathized with each other: mean (*'I empathized*

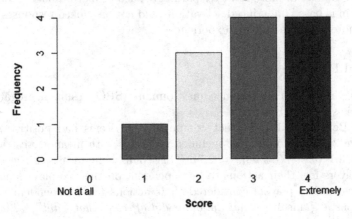

Fig. 9. Frequency bar plot of answers to the item *'I felt inclined to work together with the other'*.

with the other') $= 2.6$ and found it fairly enjoyable to be with the other: mean (*'I found it enjoyable to be with the other'*) $= 2.8$.

For the Psychological Involvement - Negative Feelings component, the overall mean score was negative (mean under 2). Players only slightly indicated negative feelings towards the other ($\overline{neg.feelings} = 0.9$). This component included five items with mean scores ranging from 0.3 to 1.6. Players didn't feel jealousy: mean (*'I felt jealous about the other'*) $= 0.3$ or revengeful towards the other player at all: mean (*'I felt revengeful'*) $= 0.4$. On the other hand, players felt moderately influenced by the other's moods: mean (*'I was influenced by the other's moods'*) $= 1.6$.

The question *'I felt inclined to work together with the other'* was added to the questionnaire as a measure of intention to cooperate among the players. Results show that the majority of players (8 out of 12) gave the item a score of 3 or 4, agreeing 'fairly' or 'extremely' with the sentence (see Fig. 9). The mean score for this item was 2.9, which means that overall, players felt 'fairly' inclined to work together with the other player. These results suggest that Kessel Run met the requirements proposed in Sect. 2.1 for good cooperative game design.

5   Conclusions

In this paper we have presented a novel BCI game, Kessel Run, developed with the intention of breaching the gap between fun games and BCI games. We developed Kessel Run as a multiplayer BCI game by following good game design practices and implementing mechanics that suited the SSVEP control paradigm, as well as taking into account the sociability aspect between players. Our goal is for Kessel Run to be played outside the laboratory, and as such we implemented it using flexible software that supports multiple BCI devices, using only 2 EEG electrodes and with a short training period required.

The game is a space exploration race, in which the 2 players must cooperate with one another in the steering of a spaceship in order to dodge asteroids and survive for 2 min in space without losing all fuel. For the ship steering, cooperative mechanics that are suited for the BCI paradigm were implemented.

Kessel Run was played by 12 participants and rated for game experience and social presence. We grouped questionnaire responses into their key items and evaluated player SSVEP performance.

While SSVEP might not be a reliable paradigm to control the Kessel Run game (only a maximum of 79% accuracy for a 33% chance level was achieved), some changes could be made in future game iterations in order to improve its performance. Using a checkerboard pattern instead of a simple flickering LED square could have given stronger SSVEPs responses [19]. We could also resort to machine learning algorithms to improve SSVEP classification, but these might have higher computation costs and could potentially be slower, which is the reason they were not used in this project. In contrast, using motor imagery instead of the SSVEP paradigm could lead to a more intuitive and perhaps reliable control, although at the expense of longer training sessions and possible BCI illiteracy [18].

Regarding Kessel Run's game experience and overall successfulness in the application of good game design practices, we looked into the reported user experience to find that despite SSVEP's low performance, Flow was still achieved as players felt challenged by the game (see Fig. 7). We believe that following the design requirements in Kessel Run helped in creating an enjoyable and positive experience to its players.

As a multiplayer game between two co-located players, we looked into the social presence felt while playing Kessel Run, investigating psychological and behavioral involvement (see Fig. 8). In general, players considered their actions fairly dependent on the other's actions. In a cooperative game, this behavioral involvement results from the game having collaborative tasks and players having inter-dependent roles, design requirements established in Sect. 2.1. The majority of players indicated in fact they felt fairly to extremely inclined to work together with the other (see Fig. 9), as should be in a collaborative game. Players empathized with the other and found it fairly enjoyable to play the game together, even though they did not particularly admire the other. Negative feelings were generally very low with players only reporting they were slightly influenced by the other's moods but didn't feel jealous or revengeful towards the other player at all.

Despite its shortcomings in the BCI performance, with this work we intend to draw attention to the importance of good game design in BCI games. BCIs are a naturally challenging way of control and therefore require extra care when applied to gaming. By developing unique game mechanics and taking the user experience into consideration we expect to encourage the creation of new multi-player games in the BCI gaming field.

Acknowledgments. We would like to express our gratitude to the Erasmus+ programme for its student mobility funding.

References

1. Choi, K., Cichocki, A.: Control of a wheelchair by motor imagery in real time. In: Fyfe, C., Kim, D., Lee, S.-Y., Yin, H. (eds.) IDEAL 2008. LNCS, vol. 5326, pp. 330–337. Springer, Heidelberg (2008). https://doi.org/10.1007/978-3-540-88906-9_42
2. Guan, C., Thulasidas, M., Wu, J.: High performance P300 speller for brain-computer interface. In: IEEE International Workshop on Biomedical Circuits and Systems. IEEE (2004)
3. Ahn, M., Lee, M., Choi, J., Jun, S.: A review of brain-computer interface games and an opinion survey from researchers, developers and users. Sensors **14**(8), 14601–14633 (2014)
4. Reuderink, B., Nijholt, A., Poel, M.: Affective pacman: a frustrating game for brain-computer interface experiments. In: Nijholt, A., Reidsma, D., Hondorp, H. (eds.) INTETAIN 2009. LNICST, vol. 9, pp. 221–227. Springer, Heidelberg (2009). https://doi.org/10.1007/978-3-642-02315-6_23
5. Tangermann, M., Krauledat, M., Grzeska, K., Sagebaum, M., Blankertz, B., Vidaurre, C., Müller, K.-R.: Playing pinball with non-invasive BCI. In: NIPS, pp. 1641–1648 (2008)
6. Pires, G., Torres, M., Casaleiro, N., Nunes, U., Castelo-Branco, M.: Playing Tetris with non-invasive BCI. In: IEEE 1st International Conference on Serious Games and Applications for Health (SeGAH), pp. 1–6. IEEE (2011)
7. Spil Games: State of Online Gaming Report. Spil Games (2013)
8. Hjelm, S.I., Browall, C.: Brainball-using brain activity for cool competition. In: Proceedings of the First Nordic Conference on Computer-Human Interaction (NordiCHI), Stockholm, Sweden, p. 9 (2000)
9. Bonnet, L., Lotte, F., Lécuyer, A.: Two brains, one game: design and evaluation of a multiuser BCI video game based on motor imagery. In: IEEE Transactions on Computational Intelligence and AI in Games, pp. 185–198 (2013)
10. Gürkök, H., Nijholt, A., Poel, M., Obbink, M.: Evaluating a multi-player brain-computer interface game: challenge versus co-experience. Entertain. Comput. **4**(3), 195–203 (2013)
11. Maby, E., Perrin, M., Bertrand, O., Sanchez, G., Mattout, J.: BCI could make old two-player games even more fun: a proof of concept with "connect four". In: Advances in Human-Computer Interaction (2012)
12. Gürkök, H., Nijholt, A., Poel, M.: Brain-computer interface games: towards a framework. In: Herrlich, M., Malaka, R., Masuch, M. (eds.) ICEC 2012. LNCS, vol. 7522, pp. 373–380. Springer, Heidelberg (2012). https://doi.org/10.1007/978-3-642-33542-6_33
13. Sweetser, P., Wyeth, P.: GameFlow: a model for evaluating player enjoyment in games. Comput. Entertain. **3**(3), 3 (2005)
14. Csikszentmihalyi, M.: Flow: The Psychology of Optimal Experience. Harper Perennial, New York City (1990)
15. Salen, K., Zimmerman, E.: Rules of Play: Game Design Fundamentals. MIT Press, Cambridge (2004)

16. van Veen, G.: Brain invaders-finding the paradox of control in a P300-game through the use of distractions. Master's thesis, University of Twente, The Netherlands (2013)

17. Wendel, V., Gutjahr, M., Göbel, S., Steinmetz, R.: Designing collaborative multi-player serious games: escape from Wilson Island - a multiplayer 3D serious game for collaborative learning in teams. Educ. Inf. Technol. **18**(2), 287–308 (2013)

18. Guger, C., Daban, S., Sellers, E., Holzner, C., Krausz, G., Carabalona, R., Gramatica, F., Edlinger, G.: How many people are able to control a P300-based Brain-Computer Interface (BCI)? Neurosci. Lett. **462**(1), 94–98 (2009)

19. Vialatte, F.-B., Maurice, M., Dauwels, J., Cichocki, A.: Steady-state visually evoked potentials: focus on essential paradigms and future perspectives. Prog. Neurobiol. **90**(4), 418–438 (2010)

20. van de Laar, B., Gürkök, H., Plass-Oude Bos, D., Poel, M., Nijholt, A.: Experiencing BCI control in a popular computer game. IEEE Trans. Comput. Intell. AI Games **5**(2), 176–184 (2013)

21. Tello, R.M.G., Muller, S.M.T., Bastos-Filho, T., Ferreira, A.: A comparison of techniques and technologies for SSVEP classification. In: 5th ISSNIP-IEEE Biosignals and Biorobotics Conference: Biosignals and Robotics for Better and Safer Living (BRC), pp. 1–6 (2014)

22. BCI2000 Wiki (2017). http://bci2000.org/wiki/User_Reference:Matlab_MEX_Files

23. IJsselsteijn, W., De Kort, Y., Poels, K.: The game experience questionnaire: development of a self-report measure to assess the psychological impact of digital games (2013, manuscript in preparation)

24. De Kort, Y., Poels, K., IJsselsteijn, W.: Digital games as social presence technology: development of the social presence in gaming questionnaire (SPGQ). In: Proceedings of PRESENCE, pp. 1–9 (2007)

25. Hakvoort, G., Reuderink, B., Obbink, M.: Comparison of PSDA and CCA detection methods in a SSVEP-based BCI-system. Technical report TR-CTIT-11-03, Centre for Telematics and Information Technology University of Twente (2011)

26. Allison, B.Z., McFarland, D.J., Schalk, G., Zheng, S.D., Jackson, M.M., Wolpaw, J.R.: Towards an independent brain-computer interface using steady state visual evoked potentials. Clin. Neurophysiol. **119**(2), 399–408 (2008)

Persuasive Games for Intergenerational Social Interaction in Urban Environments

Mark Mushiba(✉), Vincenzo D'Andrea, and Antonella De Angeli

University of Trento, Via Sommarive, 9, 38123 Povo, TN, Italy
{mark.mushiba,vincenzo.dandrea,
antonella.deangeli}@unitn.it

Abstract. Social isolation in urban areas is a societal challenge. It affects people of all ages but particularly elderly who struggle to maintain social ties into later-life. Interventions in social isolation primarily focus on elderly in clinical care, overlooking the existence of older adults who live independently. Despite facing dwindling social contact, groups of healthy older adults reside alongside large groups of younger citizens that might offer much needed social interaction. This type of intergenerational social interaction seems promising but motivations of elderly to engage with younger groups who are not necessarily related to them are not well-understood and vice-versa. Persuasive games have the potential to encouraging social interaction. This paper presents a preliminary work on investigating motivations for intergenerational interaction rooted in persuasion theory. It proposes the use of the Integrated Behavior Model as a theoretical framework for understanding behavioral determinants and explores the use of games as a way of fostering changes in attitudes that could enhance intergenerational interactions.

Keywords: Older adults · Intergenerational games · Persuasive games
Active ageing

1 Introduction

Urban areas- towns, cities and their suburbs are home to nearly three quarters of the European Union's population [1]. This supports the notion that citizens, national and foreign urban migrants will work and age in cities. Although the problem of ageing is often included in city plans such as smart city concepts, these visions usually only take infrastructural and mobility needs of older people into account. The infrastructural needs are provided for by augmenting spaces to make them "age-friendly", in other words fulfilling the assistive needs of older adults related to decline in physical and cognitive abilities [2]. Although urban areas should always cater to the mobility needs of older adults, it is also important to meet their social needs [2]. Recent studies show sustained social interaction to be a stronger predictor of successful ageing than mental and physical conditions [3]. While the link between social interaction and a higher quality of life is not always clear, the benefits of social interactions are generally presented as counters to the negative effects of social isolation. It has been reported that social isolation leads to higher cases of dementia, depression and other health

© ICST Institute for Computer Sciences, Social Informatics and Telecommunications Engineering 2018
Y. Chisik et al. (Eds.): INTETAIN 2017, LNICST 215, pp. 96–104, 2018.
https://doi.org/10.1007/978-3-319-73062-2_7

conditions that expedite the need for institutional care [4]. The increasing need to care for older adults is often implicated as one of the stressors of economic resources in urban growth plans [12].

Information Technology (IT)-based interventions have emerged as promising tools for supporting the lives of older adults in cities. These interventions focus on how IT can enhance the social lives of older adults in a way that enables them to live independently for as long as possible [5]. For instance, monitoring applications use wearable sensors to track the physical state of a user and notify caregivers in case of abnormalities without requiring the user to leave their home [5]. In spite of the benefits it may provide, it is clear that exploiting IT for monitoring can contribute to further social isolation. This undesired effect might be associated to mainstream views of technology which consider older adults as a passive, frail, isolated group that is separated from the larger part of society [3, 6].

We find the view of older adults as an isolated group surprising since the reality is that there are populations of healthy older adults who live independently in city neighborhoods alongside younger groups of citizens. We view this current limited perspective of older adults as a missed opportunity to foster interactions between these different groups. Intergenerational social interaction can address the issue of social isolation, but current challenges to realizing this vision may be attitudinal [2, 7, 8], reflecting a diffuse in *ageism*. Ageism is often presented as negative attitudes younger and older people may hold towards each other [9]. Younger people may view older people as frail and unproductive while older people may regard younger people as troublesome and unruly [3]. There is growing interest in the use of games to promote prosocial behavior between younger and older people. Similar to other research [7, 10], we posit that the success of efforts in intergenerational play requires a keen investigation into motivations and other determinants to engage in this kind of interaction. We propose the use of the Integrated Behavior Model as a theoretical framework for understanding behavioral intentions around intergenerational interaction. We further maintain that grounding intergenerational play in persuasive theory can potentially enhance its goals, particularly for interactions between non-familial players. In the following sections, we introduce a series of concepts related to the problem of social isolation in elderly and propose a research approach towards addressing it.

2 Related Work

2.1 Intergenerational Approach to Social Isolation

As the world's ageing population continues to grow the need for medical care is likely to increase. Furthermore, the rise in the ageing population has been accompanied by a rise in social isolation, a condition of minimal involvement in social life that can lead to feelings of loneliness, depression and dementia [11]. A large part of research has addressed social isolation attempting to increasing communications between older adults and their families or within same age peers [3, 5]. Intergenerational interactions within families have been shown to have positive effects on the psychological well-being of both younger and older people [3]. While these benefits are widely elaborated on, there is very little research that elaborates on how intergenerational interaction can be improved in the broader society. Studies suggest that there seems to be a diffuse problem of social disengagement between older and younger people of no relation [3] where the motivations to create or maintain social attachments are less apparent. This breakdown is likely to be more relevant in urban areas that include larger populations of unrelated individuals [12]. While some people may regard the separation between younger and older people as natural, we see it as a problem that worsens social isolation and wastes the opportunity to foster new relationships between people who live side by side. Previous research in intergenerational interaction [13] show that elderly people reported a more positive attitude towards younger people and vice-versa [14] after intergenerational engagements. It is hardly surprising that there has been a movement to extend these benefit using games. While this game-based intergenerational approach has clear benefits, there is need for a more coherent effort in improving attitudes between players of a different generation and relation.

2.2 Persuasive Games

Persuasive technology (PT) is a term used to describe systems that are designed to influence a user's behavior or attitude without coercion [15]. By extension, persuasive games try to accomplish the same goals by gameplay. Games have crossed over from being used purely for entertainment and have also become a medium for tackling complex societal issues [16]. The use of games as behavior and attitude change agents is significantly elaborated on by Bogost [17]. The recent success of games like *This War of Mine* and *Spec Ops: The Line* has further renewed interest in the use of games as tools of persuasion [16] and it is not surprising that digital games have also been identified as a viable means to promote social interaction and learning between different age groups [3, 10]. The use of games is further bolstered by the increase in the number of gamers over the age of 50 [18].

While games, and more broadly gameful experiences, follow a characteristic of being rule-based and structured [19], persuasion can also be implemented in playful experiences. According to Deterding et al. [19], playful experiences fall in the region of care-free play where activities support a more exploratory, free-from, expressive, improvisational amalgamation of meanings and behaviors. Kors et al. [16] elaborate on the potential of playful experiences to influence attitude formation and in the long run, behavior change. Although distinctions have been drawn between game and play [19], we do not see the need to introduce a new definition for a combination of the two. Instead we use the term "gameful experiences" to mean a combination of both rule-based goal oriented structure of traditional games and the open exploratory modes of play. This mix of game and play is especially important as it allows for prototyping play modes and investigating motivations, it does so by presenting open modes of play that encourage discovery and iterative design while maintaining a light-weight structure of game rules. Gameful experiences can be facilitated without the more committed investment required to play long complex narrative-driven digital games and therefore, may even be more successful at recruiting reluctant players.

There are several mechanisms used to implement persuasion in game and play, these include but are not limited to enjoyment, immersion (engagement), flow, procedural rhetoric and persuasive strategies. The mechanisms are interdependent and contribute to promoting positive reflection and engagement in the case of attitudes. Of the five that we have listed, we find enjoyment, procedural rhetoric and persuasive strategies to be the most relevant. Enjoyment can be loosely described as the qualities of a product that make it fun or pleasurable to use [20]. Fun is distinct from pleasure in that it is associated with distraction and leisure, while pleasure is associated with absorption brought about by skill, challenge and clear goals [20]. Both fun and pleasure are important to enjoyment and may be cultivated to bring about different levels of enjoyment in a game [20]. Although it hasn't always been at the center of games with a purpose, researchers have prioritized enjoyment to be instrumental to all other goals games might hope to achieve [18, 21]. Procedural rhetoric refers to the way games use processes persuasively by guiding players through different stages of reflection [17]. Guiding players through processes in a game has been shown to produce strong feelings of empathy and attitude change towards groups or individuals [16, 17]. Persuasive strategies can be thought of as principles adapted from social psychology that explain why people comply, perform or reject certain behaviors [22]. The *authority* persuasive strategy, for instance, refers to the tendency for people to easily comply to requests made by people we regard as having advanced knowledge on a specific topic [23]. All the mechanisms discussed are used to strengthen the persuasive quality of a game.

2.3   Integrated Behavior Model

In trying to understand the factors that affect persuasive interventions, researchers often rely on psychological frameworks [22, 24]. The frameworks are useful for examining behavioural determinants, which are the casual factors that explain why a behaviour is likely to be adopted or rejected. While some designers may consider behavioural determinants before a design, it is common for designers to engage in design without the guide of a theoretical framework [24]. Nevertheless, it has been suggested that following a theory-based design of persuasive systems leads to higher success [24]. Several models such as the Fogg Behavior Model [15] and the Attitudinal Gameplay Model [16] have been proposed to design persuasive systems building on psychological frameworks. These abstractions have the advantage of being simple but they may lack the complexity required to understand the relationship between behavioural determinants and persuasive goals. The Integrated Behavior Model is a framework that describes a given behaviour as a function of attitudes, perceived norms and personal agency [25]. The *attitude* reflects a person's predisposition to a certain behavior. The *perceived norm* describes the influence of others to perform (or not to perform) a behavior. The *personal agency* influences the extent to which a person's ability or environmental factors enable them to perform the behavior. We believe the IBM has the potential to overcome the challenges of conventional persuasive design, especially where persuasive design oversimplifies behavioural determinants in favour of being efficient [26].

3   Proposed Approach to Persuasive Games for Intergenerational Interaction

The possible state of opposing attitudes between older adults and younger citizens leads us to consider persuasive games and persuasive gameful experiences as a potential way of facilitating intergenerational social interaction. This section describes the research we intend to carry out to accomplish the research goal of developing a persuasive game for intergenerational interaction. Furthermore, we also aim to develop a framework that shows how persuasive strategies, procedural rhetoric and enjoyment can be used to enhance attitudes in the frame of a game. We use the research through design process [27] to probe the concepts of game and play, and plan to evaluate technical artifacts that encompass our learning. Figure 1 illustrates our research process, starting with an examination of behavioral determinants, the design of persuasive gameful experiences and finally, an evaluation of player experience. The process unfolds incrementally and iteratively, building towards a final technical artifact.

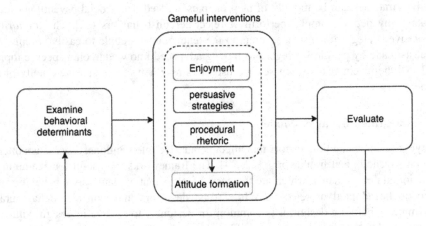

Fig. 1. Research design

3.1   Behavioral Determinants

While there have been a considerable number of efforts in the direction of intergenerational interventions, most interventions using games have received minimal attention outside the family sphere [3, 7]. We aim to investigate the motivations for non-familial intergenerational interaction, why and if older and younger players would choose to engage with the other in play. This is a distinctive aspect of our research. Furthermore, intergenerational games have partly been unsuccessful due to the little attention given to behavioral determinants. Looking at the broader context of persuasive games, Kors et al. [16] state that current persuasive design practices rarely consider how attitudes are formed. This point is particularly significant since change in attitude is considered as a reliable predictor of intent for behavior change [16]. Kors et al. [16] further point out that although there is enough evidence to demonstrate the persuasive power of games, there is little in the way of research that practically shows how persuasion and therefore behavioral determinants can be accounted for in the implementation of persuasive games. It is from these shortcomings that we have chosen a behavior-theory driven approach that identifies behavioral determinants and reconciles them with persuasive strategies in the frame of games and play.

As shown in Fig. 1 the first part of our research is concerned with investigating the behavioral determinants for non-familial interaction. This will involve a closer look at motivations, perceived norms, self-efficacy and attitudes. We plan to carry out semi-structured interviews for this part of the research. The target of the initial studies will be older adults that live independently (60 < older) and youth (18–30) residing in Trento, Italy. Through means of a conceptual design, prior work by [26] used the IBM to study the motivations of older adults to use a social network that connects older adults with similar interests. Within the IBM framework that considers three major components (attitudes, perceived norms and self-efficacy), a series of semi-structured interviews were carried out. The results showed a diversity in the motivations of older adults which are only partly met by the medical model that dominates the design of older adult technologies [26]. Although the objective of the early research had no specific focus on games, the results provide valuable insights on behavioral determinants that might be useful in the design of a persuasive game intervention. We intend to expand on the use of the IBM for technology design by using it to study the determinants of older adults and younger participants towards intergenerational interaction. Finally, we also intend to probe the meaning of game and play, which can illuminate how these concepts differ across generations.

3.2 Gameful Interventions

As is typical of any research through design project, we do not immediately envision developing a final commercially-ready artefact. Instead we rely on capturing multiple perspectives of the problem, generating ideas and prototyping a series of game and play experiences. That said, we do however expect that we will have an artefact of relatively high fidelity that will encompass most of the learnings from earlier iterations. It may be called a final artefact in that sense. The technical artefacts will be developed through participatory practice with older and younger players. We choose this form of co-creative design to record player sensibilities and to develop play mechanics, dynamics and aesthetics of the gameful experiences. Similar studies [28] affirm that a participatory approach can be effective for finding a good balance of game features for both player types. Involving both younger and older players will also provide a platform to playtest the gameful experiences. Once again we harken back to the idea of using gameful experiences as instantiations of game and play that build knowledge around the quality of the interactions, behavioral intentions and the effectiveness of persuasive strategies. We feel that this approach is useful to balance aspects of purpose and play that would otherwise be lost in creating a fully-fledged game for entertainment or a purpose game that misses out on the crucial aspects of enjoyment that make games fun to play. We expect to investigate the interplays between enjoyment, persuasive strategies, procedural rhetoric, and how they affect attitude formation.

3.3 Evaluation

We constrain our evaluation to co-located play, for the simple reason that remote play is disembodied while co-located play utilizes presence and direct interpersonal engagement. Here we make an assumption that co-located play might be better at promoting social interaction than remote play where players can easily disengage [29]. We evaluate the quality of interactions using observation, post-game questionnaires, and pre and post interviews. This approach has been used by other researchers [10, 16] in assessing attitude change. Due to the fact that the persuasive goal is a change or reinforcement of attitudes, we are reluctant to operationalize measures such as a "performance of target behavior". We feel instead that focusing on the self-reported gameful experiences would offer greater depth in understanding the efficacy of the interventions. In our evaluation we look at the quality of the interactions but we also examine how the gameful interventions enhance determinants. An incremental and iterative approach to the research ensures that the learning outcomes of each iteration inform the properties of the next, all the while improving our knowledge of both determinants and persuasive mechanisms (see Fig. 1).

4 Discussion and Future Work

Our research aims to investigate the determinants for intergenerational interaction among urban citizens (of no relation) for the purpose of designing persuasive gameful experiences that addresses social isolation concerns. We are currently applying research through design inquiry methods to understand the state of attitudes between potential young and older adult players. The results of these preliminary studies, review of existing literature and a participatory workshop will inform the design of persuasive games that will be evaluated with the target users. An additional point of interest in our research is to investigate the role of fun in the effectiveness of persuasive games. On the one hand, persuasive design seems to offer a way to improve the persuasive quality of games, on the other hand it seems like too much of an emphasis on persuasion can distract from the more engaging qualities of games. We also hope to show the distinct advantages that non-familial interactions provide over the more established familial convention.

References

1. European Union: Urban Europe statistics on cities, towns and suburbs: 2016 Edition. EU (2016)
2. Righi, V., Sayago, S., Blat, J.: Urban ageing: technology, agency and community in smarter cities for older people. In: Proceedings of the 7th International Conference on Communities and Technologies. ACM (2015)
3. Zhang, F., Kaufman, D.: A review of intergenerational play for facilitating interactions and learning. Gerontechnology 14(3), 127–138 (2016)
4. Baecker, R., Sellen, K., Crosskey, S., Boscart, V., Barbosa Neves, B.: Technology to reduce social isolation and loneliness (2014)

5. Parra, C., Silveira, P., Far, I.K., Daniel, F., De Bruin, E.D., Cernuzzi, L., D' Andrea, V., Casati, F.: Information technology for active ageing: a review of theory and practice. Interaction 7(4), 351–448 (2013)
6. Giaccardi, E., Kuijer, K., Neven, L.: Design for resourceful ageing: intervening in the ethics of gerontechnology (2016)
7. Thang, L.L.: Promoting intergenerational understanding between the young and old: the case of Singapore. In: UN Report of the Expert Group Meeting in Qatar, March 2011
8. Giles, H., Ryan, E.B., Anas, A.P.: Perceptions of intergenerational communication across cultures: young people's perceptions of conversations with family elders, non-family elders and same-age peers. J. Cross-Cult. Gerontol. 18, 1–32 (2003)
9. Williams, S., Renehan, E., Cramer, E., Lin, X., Haralambous, B.: 'All in a day's play' - an intergenerational playgroup in a residential aged care facility. Int. J. Play 1(3), 250–263 (2012). https://doi.org/10.1080/21594937.2012.738870
10. Rice, M., Tan, W.P., Ong, J., Yau, J.L, Wan, M., Ng, J.: The dynamics of younger and older adult's paired behavior when playing an interactive silhouette game (2013)
11. Naufal, R.: Addressing Social Isolation Amongst Older Victorians. Department of Planning and Community Development (2008)
12. Arup, Help Age International, Intel, Systematica, Shaping Ageing Cities: 10 European Case Studies (2015)
13. Boon, S.D., Brussoni, M.J.: Popular images of grandparents examining young adults' views of their closest grandparents. Pers. Relatsh. 5(1), 105–119 (1998)
14. Meshel, D.S., McGlynn, R.P.: Intergenerational contact, attitudes, and stereotypes of adolescents and older people. Educ. Gerontol. 30(6), 457–479 (2004)
15. Fogg, B.J.: Persuasive Technology: Using Computers to Change What We Think and Do. Morgan Kaufmann, Burlington (2003)
16. Kors, M.J.L., van der Spek, E.D., Schouten, B.A.M.: A foundation for the persuasive gameplay experience (2015)
17. Bogost, I.: Persuasive Games: The Expressive Power of Video Games. The MIT Press, Cambridge (2007)
18. De Schutter, B., Abeele, V.V.: Towards a gerontoludic manifesto. Anthropol. Aging 36(2), 112–120 (2015)
19. Deterding, S., Dixon, D., Khaled, R., Nacke, L.E.: From game design elements to gamefulness: defining "gamification". In: Proceedings of the 15th International Academic MindTrek Conference: Envisioning Future Media Environments, Mind-Trek 2011, pp. 9–15. ACM Press, New York (2011)
20. Blythe, M., Hassenzahl, M.: The semantics of fun: differentiating enjoyable experiences. In: Blythe, M.A., Overbeeke, K., Monk, A.F., Wright, P.C. (eds.) Funology: From Usability to Enjoyment, pp. 91–100. Kluwer Academic, London (2003). https://doi.org/10.1007/1-4020-2967-5_9
21. Nacke, L.E., Drachen, A., Göbel, S.: Methods for evaluating gameplay experience in a serious gaming context. Int. J. Comput. Sci. Sport 9, 1–12 (2010)
22. Oinas-Kukkonen, H.: A foundation for the study of behavior change support systems. Pers. Ubiquit. Comput. 17, 1223–1235 (2013)
23. Cialdini, R.: Influence, Science and Practice. Allyn & Bacon, Boston (2001)
24. Orji, R.O.: Designing for behavior change: a model-driven approach for tailoring persuasive technologies (2014)
25. Montano, D.E., Kasprzyk, D., Glanz, K., Rimer, B.K., Viswanath, K.: Theory of reasoned action, theory of planned behavior, and the integrated behavioral model. Health Behav.: Theory Res. Pract. (2008)

26. Cozza, M., De Angeli, A., Jovanovic, M., Tonolli, L., Mushiba, M., McNeil, M., Coventry, L.: Understanding motivations in designing for older adults. In: Proceedings of COOP 2016, Trento, Italy (2016)
27. Zimmerman, J., Forlizzi, J., Evenson, S.: Research through design as a method for interaction design research in HCI. In: Proceedings of the SIGCHI Conference on Human Factors in Computing Systems, pp. 493–502. ACM (2007)
28. Rice, M., Cheong, Y.L., Ng, J., Chua, P.H., Theng, Y.L.: Co-creating games through intergenerational design workshops. In: Proceedings of the Designing Interactive Systems Conference, pp. 368–377 (2012)
29. Lin, X., Kang, K., Li, C., Hu, J., Hengeveld, B., Rauterberg, M., Hummels, C.: ViewBricks: a participatory system to increase social connectedness for the elderly in care homes (2016)

Trampoline Jumping with a Head-Mounted Display in Virtual Reality Entertainment

Marcel Tiator, Okan Köse, Roman Wiche, Christian Geiger[✉],
and Fritz Dorn

Mixed Reality and Visualization, University of Applied Sciences Düsseldorf,
Münsterstr 156, 40476 Düsseldorf, Germany
geiger@hs-duesseldorf.de

Abstract. Using a trampoline as a natural 3D user interface with a head-mounted display for virtual reality entertainment is a novel and challenging task. High latencies between interaction and feedback or inaccurate tracking of the user's movement can lead to simulator sickness. In the scope of this project we identified the most appropriate solutions for the described challenge by testing multiple tracking and virtual reality technologies. A fast and precise network-based system was developed using OptiTrack as a tracking solution and Samsung GearVR as a Head-Mounted Display. The introduced system offers an interface to control an application with a trampoline by providing methods to request e.g. the average jump duration or the user's current jump height. In addition, it handles interactions or changes the virtual jump height mapping. Two prototypes were developed, exemplary implementing the interface in gaming experiences. The first application was built to test possible simulator sickness with the Simulator Sickness Questionnaire conducted by 38 users during an in-house exhibition. This evaluation revealed that our system enables a safe and fascinating jumping experience without specific simulator sickness. The second application was built after the initial test to create a more entertaining Trampoline VR application.

Keywords: 3D user interface · Trampoline · Virtual reality
Head mounted display · Prototyping · User tracking

1 Introduction

The arising of high-quality Head-Mounted Displays (HMD) like the Oculus Rift CV and the HTC Vive for non-expert users strengthens the interest in virtual reality (VR) applications. Previous HMD applications often restricted the user's input to gamepads, joysticks or keyboard and mouse. Today's HTC Vive and Oculus touch controllers already enhance the VR experience significantly by providing more natural interactions as the user can use his body movements to interact with the virtual environment. Despite this, we also think that multiple other novel and promising input devices might provide different exciting experiences for users. One such novel input device for VR HMD applications might be a trampoline, since jumping on a trampoline would be an intuitive input for a variety of people, regardless of age. Our goal is to

© ICST Institute for Computer Sciences, Social Informatics and Telecommunications Engineering 2018
Y. Chisik et al. (Eds.): INTETAIN 2017, LNICST 215, pp. 105–119, 2018.
https://doi.org/10.1007/978-3-319-73062-2_8

combine the fun and excitement of this intuitive interaction with state-of-the-art HMD and tracking technologies. Therefore, the experience could be visually enhanced by virtually transporting the user to a more intriguing place like the moon. Additionally, gaming components could be added to the experience to motivate on exercising jumping.

In this work, we present a novel user interface for VR HMD experiences. For this an interface was developed under certain design criteria to control user interactions in the virtual world with a trampoline. This work is structured as follows: First, related work which have already integrated a trampoline as a 3D user interface for virtual worlds are introduced. We describe how our approach differs from the existing projects and illustrate our application and design. At the end, findings gained during an evaluation with 38 participants are discussed and concluded.

2 Related Work

Several contributions discuss trampolines as 3D input devices for virtual content. A well-known approach from the field of 3D user interfaces is JoyMan, an input device for leaning-based navigation techniques [30]. It was designed by mounting a stand on the flexible area of a trampoline. The user can lean towards a direction and moves into this direction in the virtual world. This "Human Joystick" metaphor and the simple mechanical setup provides an immersive and entertaining interface for virtual loco-motion using a mini-trampoline as input device [29]. However, JoyMan does not track jumping activities and gestures.

Shiratori et al. [6, 7, 11] developed a system to control a virtual environment with a mini trampoline. The virtual content was displayed with two projectors on the wall in front of the user. For user interaction recognition, Position Sensitive Detectors (PSD) installed beneath the trampoline measured the distance to the trampoline surface. With these measurements, they could derive user interactions like standing, walking or jumping. This way, the user could navigate through a virtual city. This VR system enhanced the motivation for exercises on the trampoline.

In contrast to Shiratori et al. [6, 7, 11], Holsti et al. [3, 4] used a bigger trampoline and the Microsoft Kinect to track user interactions. Instead of a projector, the content was displayed on a monitor to provide visual feedback for the user. They built multiple prototypes to test their system. One application integrated the Kinect camera image to cut the real video input of the user into a virtual scene. In this scene, the user could playfully practice vertical jumping techniques by reaching higher placed virtual platforms. Besides these research projects we also found footage of the game "Kinect Sports" being played with a mini trampoline [1].

Further, [12] created a trampoline jumping simulation for the Oculus Rift DK2. Nevertheless, fast accelerations such as in a jumping simulation without actual movement of the user could often lead to simulator sickness [2, 13].

To our knowledge, there are no other approaches incorporating a trampoline as an input device for VR applications that are experienced with head-mounted devices and full-body tracking.

Among other things, Frinkelstein et al. showed that jumping in VR in a three-sided CAVE can be a movement motivation for people with autism [14]. They developed a so called exergame in which the user must avoid objects that fly towards him. Another motivating VR exergame was developed in [16]. Children with cerebral palsy should do exercises with and without virtual reality. The results indicated that fun, measured by a visual analogue scale, repetitions and range of motion was higher with VR. [14, 16] showed that children can profit from VR exergames but there also projects that focus on exergames for elderly players [22, 23]. Both projects showed that games can be motivating.

In contrast to the above-mentioned CAVE-based exergames, [15] developed a HMD-based VR exergame. They attached a bicycle to a bike trainer and let the user cycle down to a virtual suburban street. With gesture input detected by a Microsoft Kinect, the user must throw newspaper into neighbourhood mailboxes. Basis for such an exergame could be design guidelines specified by [17, 19]. Interestingly, [17] interpret the criteria of immersion of gameflow [18] in exergames, such that players should control the game with their movements to achieve a high immersion. Additionally, the user should perceive appropriate feedback [18]. In a VR application with body movements, like jumping on a trampoline, control and feedback could be given by a moving avatar. Similarly, [20] showed that using an avatar in a virtual world with head and body tracking can strengthen the effect being in the virtual world because changes that follow rules of everyday sensorimotor contingencies are satisfied. Finally, Frameworks like FAAST [21] make it possible to steer an avatar in conventional games through body movements. Additionally [24] mentioned that immersion could be increased when using an HMD rather than a 2D display or an expensive CAVE.

3 Application and Design

First, the design criteria for the integrated components are described. Afterwards, we elaborate on our system and application implementation.

In our approach, we wanted to integrate a trampoline as a 3D user interface for head-mounted VR systems, where the user is motivated to move. Nonetheless, the usage of a HMD for jumping interactions yields multiple challenges and must be implemented with care. Primary design requirements are: (1) optimizing low latency tracking of the user's head and sufficient precision to enable a joyful experience without the arising of simulator sickness. Additionally, (2) the safety of the user and feeling of confidence in the system while jumping must be considered and supported. Furthermore, (3) provide sufficient multimodal feedback including a visual representation of the user based on tracking data to appropriately control jumping motions on a trampoline and increase the feeling of presence. In this work, we focus on the design and development of the basic framework to prevent simulator sickness and provide the feeling of safety for the user. The first aspect is tested by a standard questionnaire and the latter is validated by informal interviews.

3.1 Component Selection

For our use case, the two most influential components in the setup, which may produce simulator sickness, are the tracking system and the HMD. Thus, both components had to be selected with care and the requirements of the user experience in mind.

One very important aspect is to provide a wide range of user interaction space so that the user can jump on the trampoline without movement restrictions. Therefore, the tracking system must provide a sufficiently sized tracking area. This is especially important when considering elastic ropes as an addition for the trampoline, enabling an even higher jumping area for the user. Besides the enhanced jumping height, elastic ropes can provide the user a surface to grab on and enhance the sense of security when being immersed by the HMD. The visualization of the user's own body as avatar is important for the experience and has a significant impact on immersion, security and simulator sickness because it provides a more consistent view related to the real world where the user sees his body.

For the HMD, the most important properties for us were a high display frequency and resolution, as well as fast and precise head orientation tracking because of the jumping motions. However, the weight and comfort of the HMD placed also a design requirement, as the jumping motions can easily slip the HMD out of place or hurt the user on abrupt landings and can diminishing the presence in the virtual world noticeably. To quickly evaluate the possibilities, we tested different combinations of tracking systems and HMD's by ourselves (self-tests).

We started our technical development with the Oculus Rift DK2 HMD and the Microsoft Kinect v2, as the Kinect was already successfully incorporated by Holsti et al. [3, 4] for a trampoline user interface with great interaction space. Moreover, the Kinect provides a flexible markerless tracking of the whole body and gesture recognition. In our initial self-tests an avatar controlled by the Kinect tracking data mirrored the user's movement in a simple virtual environment with a trampoline reference at the ground. The benefits of a wired HMD are to access the power of a workstation to render images at a high frame rate and to ensure a fast data transport.

Aside from that, we noticed the disadvantage of dealing with the HMD cable, because the immersion is constrained by the anxiety of damaging the cable and its vibrations. In addition, during the test of the combination of Kinect's body tracking and Oculus we experienced massive headache through motion sickness, because joints can flip away and maximum sensor update rate of 30 Hz [25] from Kinect may cause high latency followed by simulator sickness while moving on the trampoline. In our mind, this solution was not appropriate for HMD VR experiences. As the cable of this solution was disruptive and the tracking was not sufficient, we expand our design criteria to use a wireless system with a more accurate tracking, such that joints will less flip away.

Hence, OptiTrack was considered as a tracking system with the Samsung S6 GearVR as a HMD, see Fig. 1. OptiTrack generally provides a wide interaction area, a high tracking frequency, low latency and sub-millimetre accuracy in an optimal setting [9]. Our OptiTrack setup included the Prime13 cameras. In contrast to the Kinect, OptiTrack requires markers on the user's body for tracking. We decided to use five rigid bodies with markers placed on the user's head, hands and feet. Thus, the user is not put through the effort of wearing a complete tracking suite. The rigid body tracking in conjunction with inverse kinematics already provides a sufficient avatar tracking for our use case.

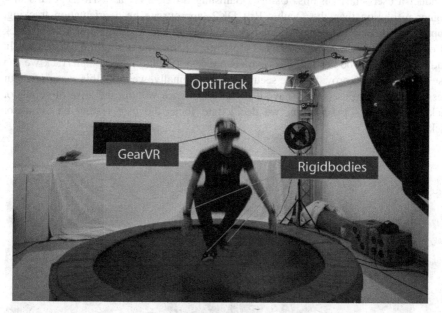

Fig. 1. Final setup: OptiTrack and GearVR. User performing interaction gesture on the trampoline by bouncing in a seating position. Fans in background are not used.

Regarding the HMD, the performance of rendering images is constrained by the smartphone's hardware and inferior to a workstation. Since OptiTrack data is transported via WLAN to the smartphone, the technical setup is fully wireless, providing greater exploration space for the user.

The Neuron Perception motion capture system combined with the Samsung S6 GearVR is another possible wireless solution, that can fit the design criteria. The suit contains multiple Inertial Measurement Units (IMUs) and sends the IMU data wireless to a workstation redirecting it to the HMD. In comparison to OptiTrack, Neuron Perception is not restricted to an area, but only to the range of the network. It is also independent of lighting conditions. As the trampoline stays indoors at a fixed position, these advantages are not relevant for our use case. Moreover, in our self-tests the tracking with Neuron Perception was less precise and had a higher latency, which is a disadvantage for the trampoline jumping scenario with HMD. The acceleration sensor of the smartphone offers another possibility to map the users jumping height. Nonetheless it is not possible to retrieve additional body movement information to map a virtual avatar. Therefore, this solution was disregarded.

In summary, we have chosen the GearVR and OptiTrack, because this setup is wireless, provides an appropriate tracking space and enables a virtual avatar representation because we can calculate body joints based on the marker tracking. During the self-test with this combination we experienced no simulator sickness but decided to conduct a user study on this. Using a Samsung S6 GearVR as a HMD results in a higher resolution than the Oculus Rift DK2, appropriate head orientation tracking, appropriate display frequency with a moderate weight and wearing comfort. OptiTrack also supported the lowest latency and most precise tracking during the self-testing. In addition, the rigid bodies and the GearVR are easy to put on. With OptiTrack we can use elastic ropes to provide more security as well. Finally, we think this system fits our design criteria and users may have a joyful experience without the arise of simulator sickness. For this publication, we decided to focus the user testing on simulator sickness.

Fig. 2. Evaluation setup with elastic ropes. User in a belt jumping in a seating position to avoid the next incoming space ship obstacle.

3.2   System Overview

The OptiTrack cameras are attached to a traverse built around the trampoline, see Fig. 1. The cameras are connected to a PC workstation running the optical motion capture software Motive to calculate positions and rotations of rigid bodies. The tracking data is sent via broadcast to the GearVR via WLAN. This data is used to control a virtual avatar based on an inverse kinematic module adapted from the Unity3D asset store. We set the origin of the virtual world coordinates at the middle of the trampoline's surface and calibrated the system with this centre. After calibration, the user has only to put on the HMD, which is already equipped with a rigid body, and one rigid body for each foot and hand. In total, we need only to track five rigid bodies to control an avatar with inverse kinematics. To initiate and start the game, the user must perform a T-pose at the centre of the trampoline. This way, the virtual avatar gets scaled and adapted to the user's proportions by considering the positions of the head, hands and feet. The whole workflow was recorded as video tutorial so that others can use the trampoline as a 3D user interface as well.

3.3 Implementation

The system was implemented with the Unity3D game engine, because it provides easy integration for multiple hardware and fast prototyping possibilities. Regarding the connection between OptiTrack and Unity3D, the implementation in [10] was integrated. However, recently OptiTrack released a Unity3D plugin themselves [8], which we would recommend for future developments.

Within Unity3D, a small framework was built to supply numerous parameters and methods to use the trampoline as a user interface. Consequently, the trampoline can easily be implemented for prototypes developed in Unity3D. First, the framework provides methods to request the current state of the user. This way, developers can check if the user is currently standing, jumping up, floating in the air, falling or landing. The framework derives these states by analysing the user's velocity and current position in relation to the initial calibration position. In addition, it is possible to retrieve various data about the user's jump. Thus, developers can request measurements like current acceleration, velocity, jump height, average jump durations, average jump heights, lowest jump or the highest jump. For instance, this data could be integrated to create high-score lists or build levels with an adjusting difficulty depending on how high the user can jump. Furthermore, the framework offers an interface to use multiple interaction features: e.g. bouncing in a seating position or running gestures while jumping. Additionally, parameters calculated by the interface can be used to create new interactions.

Besides the described data and interaction options, various perspective views and virtual avatars can be displayed. For instance, the user can switch between camera views like first person, third person, aerial perspective or a view in front of him. This offers exciting possibilities to investigate how perspectives influence the experience in VR. Moreover, diverse forms of virtual avatars can be applied. We distinguish between no avatar or avatars which have only hands and feet, full body but static, full body with fixed animation or full body with inverse kinematics. The fixed animation avatar uses the state information of the framework to play predefined animations depending on the user's current state (for instance a jumping animation is played when the user is jumping). The inverse kinematics avatar is steered by the user's hands and feet. To move the avatar's body according to the user, the head translation is used and mapped to the whole body: If the head is moving to the left, then the body is also moving to the left.

With this simplified setting, the virtual avatar gets controlled with only five markers (hands, feet and head). We found through self-tests that this method is a good approximation to map the user's movements, but it might not be appropriate for more complex movements like deforming the whole body.

3.4 Prototypes

We developed two prototypes with the system to (a) demonstrate, self-test and select different functional capabilities of the framework and (b) to test our primary requirement with this selection: to prevent simulator sickness. The first prototype was an endless-runner Jump 'N' Run game, placing the user in a lava scenery, see Fig. 3. By jumping with an offset of 25 cm from the origin to the left or right side, the user switches between three lanes. With power-ups placed in the scene, the user gains a temporary speed or jump height boost. The speed can also be raised by performing running gestures while jumping. Bouncing in a seating position resets the speed. Other gaming elements like collectable coins and flaming obstacles extends the experience. Besides switching lanes to avoid obstacles, the user can also shoot water out of his wrists to extinguish the fire obstacles.

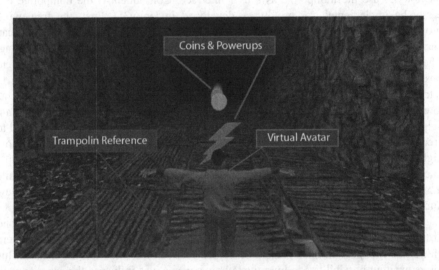

Fig. 3. Endless-runner prototype: lava scene with virtual avatar in 3rd person perspective controlled by inverse kinematics.

The second prototype immerses the user in a space scenario, see Fig. 4. In this VR experience, we added elastic ropes as a necessity for the system composition. With this setup, the user should get into a belt with elastic ropes mounted on a traverse wrapping the trampoline. Then, after an initial calibration that matches a virtual avatar to the user's body, the user plays a walk-though tutorial on how to interact in the game. Like the "avoiding space objects task" in [14], the user's task in this experience is to prevent different space ships from attacking him. This is accomplished by jumping or ducking and thus avoiding the obstacles. In addition, approaching meteoroids are collectable with hands to score points. After a certain number of meteoroids have been collected, it is possible to activate a laser beam by clapping hands together. This way, a wave of obstacles gets destroyed. A high-score for collected meteoroids and increasing the level of difficulty enhance the game and should increase motivation. The perspective view and the virtual avatar representation can be altered by swiping horizontally or vertically on the GearVR's touchpad. We added a virtual trampoline reference to the scenes, so that the user has a better feeling of orientation in the scene. Simple gestures like clapping hands and stretching the arm towards objects allow for some interactions in the scene and provide audio-visual feedback (digital effects, sound, etc.).

Fig. 4. Space prototype: jumping over incoming space ship obstacles.

4 Evaluation

We tested the space prototype during an in-house exhibition with 38 non-expert participants (Fig. 2). As we experienced in the self-tests headache, for example while jumping with Kinect and HMD, we want to explore, if persons perceive simulator sickness with our solution, containing OptiTrack and GearVR. For measuring simulator sickness, we choose the simulator sickness questionnaire (SSQ) [5] like [27, 28]. We hope to get an average score of maximum 10, this should correspond to a simulator which produces minimal symptoms [26]. Moreover, we try to create a fun experience which we, however, do not measure in this case. In each test, we helped the participant to climb into a belt attached to elastic ropes and to put on the rigid bodies and the HMD. During the game, we observed most participants making fast movements, to jump away from the space ships. It seemed like they were immersed by the game, not afraid to move and experienced a lot of fun. Depending on the participants' skill level, the duration of one game was approximately between five and eight minutes. After finishing the game, the participants answered the SSQ. They could choose none, slight, moderate and severe for each item of the SSQ (Table 1). In addition to the SSQ, we asked for the age, experience with VR, susceptibility to nausea (e.g. when driving roller coaster, same ratings as ratings of SSQ items). The users had also the opportunity to leave a comment describing the pros and cons of our application. The participants do an average of 4 (SD = 2.7) hours of sports per week. 32 people had already experience with VR. The average age of the participants was 29.3 years (SD = 8.7), ranging from 17 to 53. The average susceptibility to nausea was 0.81 (SD = 0.87). The results of the SSQ are illustrated in Fig. 5. With the weights described in [5], we obtain the mean values Nausea = 17.57, Oculomotor = 16.16, Disorientation = 29.67, Total = 22.83. Few items of the SSQ were highly rated, although participants visually seemed not to feel strong simulator sickness. For instance, we think that item 5 (difficulty focusing) could generally be highly rated due to a slightly slipping HMD during fast jumping motions.

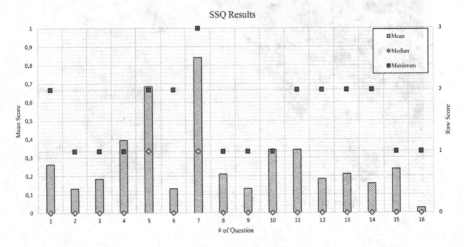

Fig. 5. SSQ results without weighting (Scores: 0 = none, 1 = slight, 2 = moderate, 3 = severe).

Table 1. Items of the SSQ [5]

# of question	Item	# of question	Item
1	General discomfort	9	Difficulty concentrating
2	Fatigue	10	Fullness of the head
3	Headache	11	Blurred vision
4	Eye strain	12	Dizziness with eyes open
5	Difficulty focusing	13	Dizziness with eyes closed
6	Salivation increasing	14	Vertigo
7	Sweating	15	Stomach awareness
8	Nausea	16	Burping

Further, participants might have increased item 7 (sweating) values because jumping on a trampoline is an inherently physically demanding activity. Some participants negatively mentioned the virtual avatar mapping. For example, they commented it like "The virtual character doesn't quite correspond with the real person.". Despite this, most of the participants had small or no criticism and did enjoy the experience greatly. They commented the application very positively with notes like "I could've actually kept playing, since I didn't feel uneasy at all. I could freely move myself and had no feeling of spatial restrictions." or "A whole new adventure thanks to the actual interaction of the body which is fully in charge. Very high fun factor.". Some participants had so much fun that they even played multiple continuous and exhausting game sessions.

5 Summary and Conclusion

In this work, we described a novel approach for HMD experience by using a trampoline as a user interface. The system benefits of the fast and precise OptiTrack tracking system and the wireless GearVR, which fit our design criteria. With this setup, we achieved an exciting experience and provided a wide interaction area for the user. It is also possible to switch between in-game references and thus to examine if an avatar is increasing the presence. In our opinion, the avatar provides more safety while moving on the trampoline, because when one jumps on the edge of the trampoline, one gets appropriate visual feedback about body location which might be not given when there is no avatar. Furthermore, we think like [20] that a self-avatar which is controlled by real tracked body movements can provide higher immersion in sense of being in the virtual environment and embodiment such that we perceive direct visual feedback to our movements. Also, Holsti et al. [3, 4] displayed the user in the game, such that user sees his own movements on the screen. Concluding that, a VR trampoline system could benefit when visualizing user's movements in the game. Although the development of the second prototype did not consider game flow criteria [18] by explicit design, it might be helpful to design games with them, when VR-applications should be joyful. We evaluated the system with the SSQ like [27, 28] and although rapid jumping motions are present and the finally score was greater than 10 we noticed most people did not feel specifically simulator sick. Reasons for a high SSQ score could be SSQ items like sweating coming from exhaustive jumping on the trampoline as sport activity. Another reason could be difficulty focussing when the HMD moves a little bit while jumping. The opinion that the participants feel low simulator sick although the SSQ score was high is strengthen by the participants' positive comments and their exhaustive movements. According to that, our system could possibly be an appropriate platform for more advanced motivating exergames. Finally, the target groups from [14, 16, 22, 23] and middle-aged people could also benefit from this work. We summarize our design decisions for an expressive VR trampoline experience as follows:

- For jumping activities and fast-moving user actions the trade-off between a high-end tethered VR device and a wireless system has been considered based on the user's actions. We decided to use a mobile setup using GearVR as the best compromise.
- For best orientation, the user's body needs to be visualized in a believable way. This requires a full-body tracking in the size of the space covered by the trampoline and of at least 5 tracking positions on the body (Head, hands, feet) if an appropriate inverse kinematic module is used. We decided to use a high-end marker-based tracking system (OptiTrack).
- Consider a minimal instrumentation of the user and provide safe play conditions. Help the user to understand the required interactions while jumping with a head-mounted VR device. We created an in-game tutorial and use elastic ropes to support this.
- Design the game based on a flexible and robust framework in a way that minimizes simulator sickness and maximizes joy of use. We designed a simple game that supports jumping activities and tested the application using a standard questionnaire for simulator sickness (SSQ). For this publication, we validated the joy of use only by self-testing and informal user feedback after the formal SSQ test.

For future work, wind machine feedback for fast-moving Jump 'N' Run games could enhance the immersion. Additionally, we would like to investigate more forms of interactions and experiences, like musical interfaces or other gaming concepts. Further, we want to study which form of avatar representations (Sect. 3.3) provides most security, embodiment, enjoyment and immersion for users. We will further investigate appropriate methods for measuring those features. As we experienced through self-tests, it is possible to use an avatar to provide system feedback to the user. It would be interesting to identify how different perspectives and avatars (Sect. 3.3) affect the interactivity and user experience. Thus, the presented work offers multiple possibilities for further user experience research.

Video

A video showing the system in action during an exhibition is available at https://vimeo.com/200660539, switch on cc to read the english text.

Selected Impressions from the System Prototype

References

1. Glenn, J.: Kinect Sports Hurdles on Trampoline for Plyometrics (2015). https://www.youtube.com/watch?v=VIxSi3stVvs
2. Google: Designing for Google Cardboard - Physiological Considerations (2016). https://goo.gl/tqqO62
3. Holsti, L., Takala, T., Martikainen, A., Kajastila, R., Hämäläinen, P.: Body-controlled trampoline training games based on computer vision. In: CHI 2013 Extended Abstracts on Human Factors in Computing Systems, CHI EA 2013, pp. 1143–1148. ACM, New York (2013)
4. Kajastila, R., Hämäläinen, P.: Motion games in real sports environments. Interactions 22(2), 44–47 (2015)
5. Kennedy, R.S., Lane, N.E., Berbaum, K.S., Lilienthal, M.G.: Simulator sickness questionnaire: an enhanced method for quantifying simulator sickness. Int. J. Aviat. Psychol. 3(3), 203–220 (1993)
6. Mori, H., Shiratori, K., Fujieda, T., Hoshino, J.: Flexible foot interface for versatile training field. In: SIGGRAPH 2009: Posters, SIGGRAPH 2009, p. 99:1. ACM, New York (2009)
7. Mori, H., Shiratori, K., Fujieda, T., Hoshino, J.: Versatile training field: the wellness entertainment system using trampoline interface. In: ACM SIGGRAPH 2009 Emerging Technologies, SIGGRAPH 2009, p. 25:1. ACM, New York (2009)
8. OptiTrack: OptiTrack Unity Plugin (2016). http://wiki.optitrack.com/index.php?title=OptiTrackUnityPlugin
9. OptiTrack-Support: General FAQ (2016). http://optitrack.com/support/faq/general.html
10. ozzyonfire: UnityOptiTrack - Github repository - A test project to get Optitrack streaming into Unity 3D without using a DLL (2014). https://github.com/ozzyonfire/UnityOptitrack
11. Shiratori, K., Mori, H., Hoshino, J.: The trampoline entertainment system for aiding exercise. In: Proceedings of the 8th International Conference on Virtual Reality Continuum and Its Applications in Industry, VRCAI 2009, pp. 169–174. ACM, New York (2009)
12. thebko: Trampolake Unity Demo for Oculus DK2 (2014). https://www.youtube.com/watch?v=y6tnnrIVwUI
13. OCULUS VR: OCULUS Best Practices (2016). https://static.oculus.com/documentation/pdfs/intro-vr/latest/bp.pdf
14. Finkelstein, S.L., Nickel, A., Barnes, T., Suma, E.A.: Astrojumper: designing a virtual reality exergame to motivate children with autism to exercise. In: 2010 IEEE Virtual Reality Conference (VR), Waltham, MA, USA. IEEE (2010)
15. Bolton, J., Lambert, M., Lirette, D., Unsworth, B.: PaperDude: a virtual reality cycling exergame. In: CHI 2014, Toronto, Ontario, Canada. ACM (2014)
16. Bryanton, C., Bossé, J., Brien, M., McLean, J., McCormick, A., Sveistrup, H.: Feasibility, motivation, and selective motor control: virtual reality compared to conventional home exercise in children with cerebral palsy. CyberPsychology Behav. 9(2), 123–128 (2006)
17. Tanaka, K., Parker, J.R., Baradoy, G., Sheehan, D., Holash, J.R., Katz, L.: A comparison of exergaming interfaces for use in rehabilitation programs and research. J. Can. Game Stud. Assoc. 6(9), 69–81 (2012)
18. Sweetser, P., Wyeth, P.: GameFlow: a model for evaluating player enjoyment in games. ACM Comput. Entertain. 3(3), Article 3A (2005). ACM
19. Sinclair, J., Hingston, P., Masek, M.: Consideration for the design of exergames. In: GRAPHITE 2007, Perth, Western Australia (2007)

20. de la Pena, N., Weil, P., Llobera, J., Giannopoulos, E., Pomés, A., Spanlang, B., Friedman, D., Sanchez-Vives, M.V., Slater, M.: Immersive journalism: immersive virtual reality for the first-person experience of news. Presence 19(4), 291–301 (2010)
21. Suma, E.A., Lange, B., Rizzo, A.S., Krum, D.M., Bolas, M.: FAAST: the flexible action and articulated skeleton toolkit. In: IEEE Virtual Reality 2011, Singapore. IEEE (2011)
22. de Bruin, E.D., Schoene, D., Pichierri, G., Smith, S.T.: Use of virtual reality technique for the training of motor control in the elderly. Zeitschrift für Gerontologie und Geriatrie 43(4), 229–234 (2010). Springer-Verlag
23. Brox, E., Luque, L.F., Evertsen, G.J.: Exergames for elderly. In: 5th International Conference on Pervasive Computing Technologies for Healthcare (PervasiveHealth) and Workshops (2011)
24. Reiners, T., Teräs, H., Chang, V., Wood, L.C., Gregory, S., Gibson, D., Petter, N., Teräs, M.: Authentic, immersive, and emotional experience in virtual learning environments: the fear of dying as an important learning experience in a simulation. In: Proceedings of the 23 Annual Teaching and Learning Forum 2014, University of Western Australia, Perth, Australia (2014)
25. Microsoft: Kinect-Hardware (2017). https://developer.microsoft.com/de-de/windows/kinect/hardware
26. Kennedy, R.S., Drexler, J.M., Compton, D.E., Stanney, K.M., Lanham, D.S., Harm, D.L.: Configural scoring of simulator sickness, cybersickness and space adaptation syndrome: similarities and differences? NASA Johnson Space Center, Houston, Texas, USA (2001)
27. Ferdous, S.M.S., Arafat, I.M., Quarles, J.: Visual feedback to improve the accessibility of head-mounted displays for persons with balance impairments. In: IEEE Symposium on 3D User Interfaces 2016, Greenville, SC, USA. IEEE (2016)
28. Fernandes, A.S., Feiner, S.K.: Combating VR sickness through subtle dynamic field-of-view modification. In: IEEE Symposium on 3D User Interfaces 2016, Greenville, SC, USA. IEEE (2016)
29. Pettré, J., Siret, O., Marchal, M., Lécuyer, A.: Joyman: an immersive and entertaining interface for virtual locomotion. In: ACM SIGGRAPH ASIA Emerging Technologies (e-Tech), Hong-Kong (2011)
30. Marchal, M., Pettré, J., Lécuyer, A.: Joyman: a human-scale joystick for navigating in virtual worlds. In: Proceedings of the IEEE Symposium on 3D User Interfaces (2011)

Exploring Children's Use of a Remotely Controlled Surfacebot Character for Storytelling

Alejandro Catala$^{(\boxtimes)}$, Mariët Theune, Dennis Reidsma, Silke ter Stal, and Dirk Heylen

Human Media Interaction, University of Twente, Enschede, The Netherlands
{a.catala, m.theune, d.reidsma,
s.terstal, d.k.j.heylen}@utwente.nl

Abstract. This paper explores the use of a remotely controlled character to be used by children in storytelling activities. The character is implemented in a moveable tablet or surfacebot, which supports the development of inexpensive expressive agents capable of moving around in real space, applicable in diverse play contexts. We carried out an exploratory study of children's interaction with an intermediate prototype. Based on the children's comments and our observations during the tests, we discuss which interaction aspects should be taken into consideration and which technical features should be further developed in a surfacebot-based storytelling system.

Keywords: Storytelling · Playful interaction · Children interaction · Robot Agent

1 Introduction

Given its inherently social and creative nature, storytelling appears to be an important activity to support children's skill development [5]. In her survey on interactive digital storytelling for children [8], Garzotto gives an overview of systems and technologies. The use of virtual intelligent characters for storytelling, relying on advanced planning techniques [16], has been an important contribution to reach outstanding levels of both narrative generation and character representation. Supporting intelligent characters beyond the computer screen and exploring opportunities to make interactive story-telling more engaging for children [1] has been gaining more interest, offering collaborative storytelling in which multiple users can participate in the activity, and including tangible objects to build a more physical storytelling environment [15]. On the move towards this physicality, which would be appropriate for mediated technology with children, these tangible objects are often toys rather than characters capable of acting autonomously, although some related work explores the use of robots as characters. Combining tangible features with virtual intelligent characters is a promising line of research that is worth exploring, as it would allow us to pick features from both realities.

© ICST Institute for Computer Sciences, Social Informatics and Telecommunications Engineering 2018
Y. Chisik et al. (Eds.): INTETAIN 2017, LNICST 215, pp. 120–129, 2018.
https://doi.org/10.1007/978-3-319-73062-2_9

The research project coBOTnity aims to make a first step towards combining physical and virtual story characters by delivering moveable touchscreen-based bots, called surfacebots, with the purpose of supporting social and collaborative playful interaction around storytelling activities with children. Rather than a system unfolding a pre-scripted story autonomously, we understand the storytelling process as a creative and dynamic activity, in which children should be able to use the mediated technology as a means of expression and collaboration. The role that surfacebots can have is an interesting issue to study due to the multiple capacities that could be implemented. The surfacebots are envisioned as *expressive agents* (through the display of the touch screen) that can *move around in physical space* (e.g., on a table). They can be controlled remotely by the child to enact parts of the story. However, being expressive agents they could also proactively contribute to the story, e.g. by expressively showing their appraisal of story events, by autonomously moving to salient places in the story space, or by otherwise responding to the story as it unfolds similar to virtual intelligent characters in screen-based interactive storytelling systems [3]. Before implementing such interactive storytelling system with intelligent surfacebots, we have developed a working prototype with some basic features to tentatively see how children might use a surfacebot in their storytelling. It allows children to use a surfacebot character controlled remotely from a tablet to express part of the story they ideate. We carried out an informal exploratory study, observing how children interacted naturally with the prototype in order to assess which technological components are most promising to be further developed.

In this paper, we discuss this study and its implications for future work. Section 2 presents some of the related work. Section 3 introduces the working prototype that was tested. Section 4 summarizes the goals, observations and remarks from the tests. Section 5 outlines immediate future work to develop the prototype further.

2 Related Work

Here we review some of the related work on playful technology with a focus on social collaboration and storytelling involving physically embodied characters or robots. Garzotto [8] gives an overview of enabling technologies and approaches to interactive storytelling for children. A strand of work focuses on how to empower children as interactive storytellers, and especially how to make the activity collaborative (e.g. [13, 20]).

Some of the related work on tangible interaction in storytelling specifically involves tabletops and related tangible objects (e.g. [2, 4, 21]). In this segment, the Interactive Storyteller described in Alofs et al. [1] has a unique position because it integrates tangible objects representing intelligent story characters as agents capable of autonomous interaction on the tabletop. This kind of intelligence is missing in previous tabletop systems. One of the limitations of the Interactive Storyteller was, however, that the tangibles could not be actuated by the software, leading to problems of consistency between the digital and the physical representation. This problem could be solved by using robots to represent the characters.

With a different concept of tangible characters, the work in progress by Wang et al. presents Cartoon [23], a device with movable limbs which supports the recording of movement in a similar way to kinetic memory. It is used as a stand for paper or card-based images placed on top. Children can create moving creatures, plan the movement of the robotic bases, and put them to walk while telling stories.

The use of robots is also explored to either represent story characters, act as storytellers, or participate as companions in the activity. Examples of robots used as characters include GENTORO [19] and RoboTale [12]. In the first, a simple radio-controlled turtle toy is controlled by children using handheld projectors. It just follows the path indicated by the user without giving any affective responses or smart behavior. RoboTale combines a child-controlled robot with physical and virtual objects for collaborative storytelling. The control is mediated by tangible cards, which are recognized by the interactive tabletop on which the activity is taking place. In [17], stories are composed of programmed behaviors for Pleo, a dinosaur robot. It stands on a tabletop which tracks fiducial markers corresponding to sequences of behaviors indicated on a tablet PC by children.

Fridin [7] presented KindSAR, a system that uses a Nao humanoid robot acting as an embodied interactive storyteller, assisting educational staff by telling prerecorded stories, and playing a social role in supporting children's literacy development and knowledge acquisition. A social robotic learning companion in a storytelling activity with children is presented in [10]. A tablet is used to display characters, and the child and the robot (tele-operated by the experimenter) engage in a turn-taking activity, exploring the range and kind of vocabulary being used [24]. Finally, Leite et al. [11] use two MyKeepon robots to explore the development of children's social skills when interacting with fully scripted interactive narratives. They let children use tablets to choose the actions of a robot at specific moments, allowing them to see the effects of their choices. The experiment resulted in higher story recall when children interacted alone rather than in groups.

The related work shows that storytelling systems for children are starting to involve some active objects or robotic technologies. Different embodiments for robots have been explored so far, each with a different range of capabilities according to Milgram's reality-virtuality continuum discussed in [6]. For instance, some have specific features such as dance or emotions, while others cannot deliver custom visual feedback but are able to use their arms to implement advanced gestures. Yet others cannot move at all, or only in a slow or clumsy way. So far, tangibles and robots have been mostly used in storytelling as either fully controlled, expressionless characters or storytellers that show some limited expressive behavior. In contrast, in our ongoing project we strive to develop physically present characters that are expressive and can provide some autonomous input in a storytelling activity.

Given the lack of affordable robotic characters, we take advantage of the wide-spread availability of tablets in learning contexts to integrate an extensible virtual agent on a tablet with a compact robotic base, with the aim of supporting future exploration of collaborative storytelling activities with robots. The following sections present a first informal evaluation of a working prototype of these 'surfacebots' to guide the further development of such an embodiment for children's play.

3 Overview of the Working Prototype

We have developed a functional prototype to start exploring how children interact with a surfacebot while using it to tell stories. The choice of the components pursues a balance in features and costs with regard to other robotic platforms, while allowing children to interact through touch input remotely with the tablets available at school. The prototype consists of a robot-tablet (surfacebot) that embodies a character (see Fig. 1). Using a moving tablet to embody a character allows us to show a digital representation of the character's facial expressions and intentions on screen while also allowing it to move around in the physical play area. However, before testing more advanced interactive features with children (e.g. self-driven and autonomous behavior in the surfacebot), we have focused on a limited version of a surfacebot character.

Fig. 1. Examples of screens on the surfacebot representing a character. Story assets are shown in the bottom left corner of the screen.

The character representation can be changed dynamically by touching the surfacebot screen (see Fig. 1 for some examples) and the surfacebot can be driven around on the tabletop by using an additional control tablet. Images of story assets, mainly understood as props, can be displayed on the surfacebot screen by selecting the corresponding items from the control tablet (see Fig. 2-a,b) as a means of facilitating children's expression. In the test described below we also provided physical versions (cards) of the story assets (see Fig. 2-c). The current prototype is implemented in

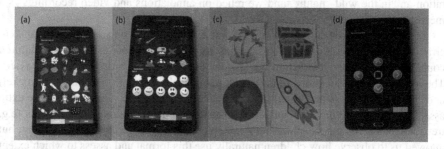

Fig. 2. Example of screens on the control tablet showing virtual story assets (a,b); physical cards showing the same assets (c); remote control (d).

Android running on 7-inch tablets. The surfacebot tablet communicates via Bluetooth with a Zumo Robot by Pololu hidden in the case to drive the movement. All tablets, either surfacebots or control, are connected via Wi-Fi through a wireless router by relying on an overlay network based on rosjava. It makes the prototype expandable, supporting multiple devices communicating commands and therefore sharing the state of interactions.

4   Exploratory Child-Surfacebot Interaction Study

We carried out an informal study of children's interaction with a surfacebot prototype to inform future development. Inspired by the most relevant aspects from the related work discussed in Sect. 2, we focused on the following aspects:

- **Storytelling**: What kind of stories do the children create with the surfacebot, and how structured are they?
- **Use of assets**: How do children use the offered physical and virtual story assets? Do we see indications that they feel the need for more or different assets?
- **Character embodiment**: Do we see indications that children see the surfacebot more like a character rather than a moving tablet used to play? Do we see indications for autonomous capacities it should have as a character?
- **Movement control**: How well do children control the surfacebot's movement? To what extent should the surfacebot move autonomously?

4.1   Context and Participants

A total of 22 children (12 male, 10 female) from 6 to 12 participated in our exploratory tests. Their parents or legal tutors provided an informed consent to participate. For logistic reasons, 13 children from 10 to 12 year-old participated on day 1 (average 10.92 y.o.), whereas 9 children from 6 to 8 participated on day 2 (average 6.7 y.o.). Their interaction with the surfacebots was one among several interactive play activities organized by the university in collaboration with visiting schools. For this reason, we followed an observational and exploratory approach rather than an experimental one, as children could decide to join our activity whenever they wished, in groups or individually, and without possibility to control for study variables. This gives the exploration an "in the wild" nature, and we relied on annotations and video recordings as a means to confirm our observations.

In our setting, we had one surfacebot and a control tablet on some tables that were arranged together to set up a flat surface. Besides the virtual story assets which children could use during their interaction we also included physical cards representing assets. The assets depicted locations (e.g., island, planet), objects (e.g., treasure map, rocket) and characters (e.g., pirate, alien) in a pirate and space domain. There were some extra assets dealing with emotions and some related to general commonplace objects (e.g. tree, ball, etc.). The physical assets did not entail any virtual feedback on the robot, but allowed us to observe how children naturally use this format and assess to which extent a mechanism should be considered to take them as interactive input.

When children joined the activity, they were explained about the robot, the controls, and assets, and they were asked to create a story with the elements given.

The older children formed a total of 4 groups, ranging from 1 to 4 members, with a mean size of 3. The younger children formed 7 groups. Four of these were actually single individuals, resulting in a mean group size of 1.57. The time spent on the activity was higher in the case of younger children. In particular, young children spent on average 7.51 min versus 5.5 min for the older groups. These numbers are informative as can be a consequence of mixed reasons (group size, age, friendship, genders, etc.) given the exploratory nature of the sessions.

4.2 Observations and Remarks

Stories

Stories took place in the context of Pirates and Space, in line with the provided assets. It was out of scope in the exploratory sessions to assess the quality of the stories told by children. However, we still made some observations on the ability of children to structure the stories being told with the surfacebot. Some groups provided high story coherence, having links between events and what they decided to happen next [22]. For example, one of the stories involved a pirate finding a boat, using it to sail to an island guided by a treasure map, and finding an empty treasure chest that made him angry. Some children had difficulties to show this kind of logically connected events. In that case, they told a story with more unconnected events, moving the robot around and picking up things. Thus, including a strategy to support the development of structure and understanding would be beneficial. For instance, by enabling the robot to give clearer feedback on consequences of actions and new states, children could be guided towards the narration of more goal-directed action sequences. Although we did not observe a clear relation between children's age and story coherence, we surmise that such support would be most beneficial for younger children who are still developing their storytelling abilities [18].

Use of assets

Both virtual and physical assets were used by the children during the storytelling activity. We observed that the physical cards were used in many cases to make sense of the space represented on the tabletop, positioning objects for the surfacebot character to find and locations to visit and thus essentially designing, on the fly, their own story world. For example, there was one episode in which the pirate found a rocket and used it to fly to Saturn to pick up the treasure; they placed a Saturn card considerably further away from where they were unfolding the story. Locations could be fairly abstract; a card with stars was used as "sky", and was referred to as a location to fly to. Cards depicting characters were sometimes used to expand the cast of characters in the story. Thus, using dolls as additional characters can be interesting.

Children had expectations of the system giving some feedback or response related to the assets. For example, when using cards placed on the tabletop, they expressed their expectation of the robot saying something related to them when driving nearby. We also observed some children showing physical cards to the robot, expecting recognition and response. When using the virtual assets, some expected sounds in addition to the visualization. One child compensated for the lack of sound from the cannon by making the sounds himself. We also observed some cases in which the children incorporated imaginary assets in their story (e.g. "the prison was demolished with a hammer", neither the prison nor hammer was provided), or adapted existing assets to their needs (e.g. "Airplane! Can't find an airplane. Oh then, I'll use a rocket"). We observed that with the physical cards, children sometimes combined assets (e.g. *an alien with a pirate hat*, or *a boat full of pirates* by joining all the pirate character cards). This kind of composition was not possible with the virtual assets, although some tried to sequence the virtual assets on screen. This triggers an important design issue, which is how to enable virtual compositions to allow children to express their ideas quickly.

Children used the offered assets as essential input for their stories, but they did not limit themselves to objects or props. Those assets representing inner states (e.g. being angry or happy) were used in both formats. Assets also triggered some reasoning. For instance, when they were discussing on where to place the Earth but using the "Mars" card for that, one of the children said "This cannot be Earth!" Thus, assets could and must be designed for educational purposes to trigger learning on new objects or concepts to leverage all the potential that an activity like this can bring.

Character embodiment

The surfacebot represented a simple character by means of a moveable tablet, capable of showing images but without any intelligent or advanced behavior. Still, children treated the character as being alive or animated, beyond a simple remotely controlled car. Observations supporting this idea are, for example, children pretending to give the robot a hug, or speaking "come to daddy".

Children could change the character. This did not only happen at the beginning to establish the main character, but also during the story to pick another character or to just change the expression of the character (e.g. the friendly pirate was changed into an angry pirate, when he did not find money in the treasure chest).

As mentioned earlier, the children expected the character to give some feedback such as sounds, in addition to visual representations. One suggestion by children was that the robot should say something when it arrives at a card or should say what it finds. Another suggestion was to have the robot ask the user to do things or give assignments. During some sessions we explored how intervening on the story by having the character make some suggestion would work. We used a second control tablet, without children being aware of it, to visualize on the robot the asset that we wanted them to use. For example, we visualized the Earth to suggest that next action could be bringing the character to Earth. This is a feature that some groups appreciated, reinforcing in their comments that they liked that "the pirate had an idea". However, children often failed to notice the robot's suggestion, which indicates that additional and different feedback (sound plus animation) is needed to inform children that there is something that the character wants them to do.

Movement control

From the children's comments immediately after the sessions as well as from our observations, we can state that driving the character is fun. Children engaged in driving the robot and it was one of the features they loved. However, we must be aware of some potential negative points. We believe that controlling the robot based on inter-active low-level commands (i.e. go forward, turn left, etc.) can take more cognitive resources than desirable and therefore could have a negative impact on the storytelling process. In this sense, a control with high level commands (i.e. "go to here", and it goes) should contribute to children having a better focus on storytelling process. None of the children suggested that the surfacebot should move autonomously; presumably because they had too much fun driving it.

5 Conclusions and Future Work

The test sessions produced a number of observations and remarks on different aspects that we have summarized above. These do not only serve as input to further develop the surfacebot-based storytelling system in our project, but would be applicable to expand similar interactive tabletop settings (e.g. [12, 17]) involving a robot and tablets as distributed controllers.

In response to our goal questions, we summarize the main points as follows. Having a surfacebot that can be controlled can help to organize events with some spatial and temporal coherence, but more support in the form of feedback must be included to scaffold the development of structure. Children managed to use assets in different ways in their stories, including more abstract concepts. We consider that virtual assets can be improved by defining feedback and robot responses, while specific tangibles or projected images on the tabletop can help in making sense of space in the story. Physical cards supported collaboration between children.

The surfacebot was treated more like an embodied character despite being remotely controlled without advanced autonomous digital features. However, children did expect to get more feedback from the robot, and they also had a positive reaction to the character proposing next steps, which is an interesting intelligent feature to be provided. We noticed that having low-level commands for movements, while it is fun, can diminish the purpose of the storytelling activity. Thus, autonomous behavior can be implemented to support the movement between locations in a higher level control. We believe that balancing or raising the interest of children in storytelling elements rather than driving the robot is important, and we must therefore ensure that driving the robot without creating a story is not possible nor takes too much cognitive effort. Towards the implementation of these improvements, we have started by integrating some function-ality of the ASAP realizer [9, 14] into the surfacebot to support animated and expressive agents, as a way to improve the character embodiment and visual feedback. We envisage that one way to tackle the fun of driving while ensuring focus on the storytelling process would be to use a location camera-based tracker relying on attached fiducial markers, so that high-level commands can be used to get the robot moving among locations. Finally, we are working on an algorithm to allow the surfacebot to make suggestions and give feedback to children based on logically connected action sequences.

With these improvements, we aim to design and carry out experiments to explore scenarios involving multiple surfacebots, investigating the usage and management of such affordable and programmable robotic characters in storytelling activities with several children.

Acknowledgements. Our thanks to the schools, teachers and children participating in the activities. Special thanks to Daniel Davison for arranging the school day trips. This project has received funding from the European Union's Horizon 2020 research and innovation programme under the Marie Sklodowska-Curie grant agreement No 701991.

References

1. Alofs, T., Theune, M., Swartjes, I.: A tabletop interactive storytelling system: designing for social interaction. Int. J. Arts Technol. **8**(3), 188–211 (2015)
2. Alves, A., Lopes, R., Matos, P., Velho, L., Silva, D.: Reactoon: storytelling in a tangible environment. In: 3rd IEEE International Conference on Digital Game and Intelligent Toy Enhanced Learning, pp. 161–165 (2010)
3. Aylett, R., Louchart, S., Dias, J., Paiva, A., Vala, M.: FearNot! - an experiment in emergent narrative. In: Intelligent Virtual Agents, pp. 305–316 (2005)
4. Cao, X., Lindley, S., Helmes, J., Sellen, A.: Telling the whole story: anticipation, inspiration and reputation in a field deployment of TellTable. In: ACM Conference on Computer Supported Cooperative Work, pp. 251–260 (2010)
5. Hall, T.: Digital renaissance: the creative potential of narrative technology in education. Creat. Educ. **3**(1), 96–100 (2012)
6. Holz, T., Dragone, M., O'Hare, G.: Where robots and virtual agents meet: a survey of social interaction. Int. J. Soc. Robot. **1**(1), 83–93 (2009)
7. Fridin, M.: Storytelling by a kindergarten social assistive robot: a tool for constructive learning in preschool education. Comput. Educ. **70**, 53–64 (2014)
8. Garzotto, F.: Interactive storytelling for children: a survey. Int. J. Arts Technol. **7**(1), 5–16 (2014)
9. Klaassen, R., Hendrix, J., Reidsma, D., op den Akker, R., van Dijk, B., op den Akker, H.: Elckerlyc goes mobile - enabling natural interaction in mobile user interfaces. Int. J. Adv. Telecommun. **6**(1&2), 45–56 (2013)
10. Kory, J., Breazeal, C.: Storytelling with robots: learning companions for preschool children's language development. In: 23rd IEEE International Symposium on Robot and Human Interactive Communication, pp. 643–648 (2014)
11. Leite, I., McCoy, M., Lohani, M., Ullman, D., Salomons, N., Stokes, C., Rivers, S., Scassellati, B.: Emotional storytelling in the classroom: individual versus group interaction between children and robots. In: 10th Annual ACM/IEEE International Conference on Human-Robot Interaction, pp. 75–82. ACM, New York (2015). https://dl.acm.org/citation.cfm?id=2696481
12. Leversund, A.H., Krzywinski, A., Chen, W.: Children's collaborative storytelling on a tangible multitouch tabletop. In: Streitz, N., Markopoulos, P. (eds.) DAPI 2014. LNCS, vol. 8530, pp. 142–153. Springer, Cham (2014). https://doi.org/10.1007/978-3-319-07788-8_14
13. Lu, F., Tian, F., Jiang, Y., Cao, X., Luo, W., Li, G., Zhang, X., Dai, G., Wang, H.: ShadowStory: creative and collaborative digital storytelling inspired by cultural heritage. In: SIGCHI Conference on Human Factors in Computing Systems (CHI 2011). ACM, New York, pp. 1919–1928 (2011)
14. Reidsma, D., van Welbergen, H.: AsapRealizer in practice – a modular and extensible architecture for a BML realizer. Entertain. Comput. **4**(3), 157–169 (2013)

15. Ribeiro, P., Iurgel, I., Ferreira, M.: Voodoo: a system that allows children to create animated stories with action figures as interface. In: Si, M., Thue, D., André, E., Lester, J.C., Tanenbaum, J., Zammitto, V. (eds.) ICIDS 2011. LNCS, vol. 7069, pp. 354–357. Springer, Heidelberg (2011). https://doi.org/10.1007/978-3-642-25289-1_47
16. Riedl, M.O., Young, R.M.: Narrative planning: balancing plot and character. J. Artif. Intell. Res. **39**, 217–267 (2010)
17. Ryokai, K., Lee, M.J., Breitbart, J.M.: Children's storytelling and programming with robotic characters. In: 7th ACM Conference on Creativity and Cognition, pp. 19–28. ACM, New York (2009)
18. Shapiro, L.R., Hudson, J.A.: Tell me a make-believe story: coherence and cohesion in young children's picture-elicited narratives. Dev. Psychol. **27**(6), 960–974 (1991)
19. Sugimoto, M.A.: Mobile mixed-reality environment for children's storytelling using a handheld projector and a robot. IEEE Trans. Learn. Technol. **4**(3), 249–260 (2011)
20. Sylla, C., Coutinho, C., Branco, P., Müller, W.: Investigating the use of digital manipulatives for storytelling in pre-school. Int. J. Child-Comput. Interact. **6**(Dec 2015), 39–48 (2015)
21. Sylla, C., Coutinho, C., Branco, P.: A digital manipulative for embodied "stage-narrative" creation. Entertain. Comput. **5**, 495–507 (2014)
22. Trabasso, T., Secco, T., van den Broek, P.: Causal cohesion and story coherence. In: Mandl, H., Stein, N.L., Trabasso, T. (eds.) Learning and Comprehension of Text, pp. 223–225. Lawrence Erlbaum Associates, Hillsdale (1982)
23. Wang, G., Tao, Y., Liu, E., Wang, Y., Yao, C., Ying, F.: Constructive play: designing for role play stories with interactive play objects. In: 9th International Conference on Tangible, Embedded, and Embodied Interaction, pp. 575–580. ACM, New York (2015)
24. Westlund, J.K., Breazeal, C.: The interplay of robot language level with children's language learning during storytelling. In: 10th Annual ACM/IEEE International Conference on Human-Robot Interaction Extended Abstracts, pp. 65–66. ACM, New York (2015)

MuMail – A Simple Multimedia Email Client

Peter Boros and Helmut Hlavacs[✉]

Entertainment Computing Research Group,
University of Vienna, Vienna, Austria
borospeterr@gmail.com, helmut.hlavacs@univie.ac.at

Abstract. Elderly people today often keep contact with their friends and relatives through modern means like email. However, email smartphone apps are often quite difficult to operate, confusing their elderly users with too many options or showing erratic behavior due to mistakes in complex swipe gestures. We developed the app MuMail especially for elderly users, which simplifies the ability to share pictures and voice-messages over email, but not text. MuMail offers a simple GUI especially designed to take away complexity. Below are described the design decisions and a preliminary evaluation of MuMail.

Keywords: Seniors · Smartphones · Share · Email · iOS
Multimedia attachments

1 Introduction

Elderly people are often scared of modern technology but more and more connect to their family and friends using email, apps, or messengers. This counteracts the fact that many elderly people live on their own and get more and more isolated due to immobility, and loss of friends. Using modern communication means thus is important to feel connected and to be part of an active community. In fact, being able to use email today turns out to be a key factor for a healthy social life for elderly people.

Though more and more seniors own smartphones, they use them differently compared to other age groups. According to a [4] a large proportion of the sample of seniors reported own a cell phone (73%), but very few used it to text messages (2.5%) or for Internet purposes (3.5%). It clearly shows that this is one area where senior citizens are well behind the total population in having and using the advanced technology. It is very similar in case of social networks. Studies show that social networks such as Facebook or Twitter do not attract elderlies at all. Even when they have Internet connection, 90% state they never use social media, and only 6% use it at least once per week. Instead, they are often confused by the complexity and functionality of communication software, and thus avoid using it. The idea of "MuMail" is to provide simple means for communication for elderly people, in order to connect them to their friends and relatives by email, without the burden of overly complex functionality. "MuMail" only allows to send and receive multimedia content as attachments, something that dominates the way elderly people communicate with their social contacts.

© ICST Institute for Computer Sciences, Social Informatics and Telecommunications Engineering 2018
Y. Chisik et al. (Eds.): INTETAIN 2017, LNICST 215, pp. 130–135, 2018.
https://doi.org/10.1007/978-3-319-73062-2_10

2   Related Work

Finding the easiest way to contact seniors with their family and friends was the fundamental motivation. The goal was to find something that would simplify the everyday life of elderly people and to provide them an effortless tool to share moments with their beloved ones.

Basically, there are three types of solutions for making complex simpler – senior apps, senior launchers and senior phones. Senior *apps* are the kind of solutions which also MuMail provides – simplified apps with just the functionality users need. Senior *launchers* change the whole smartphone GUI in such a way that elderly people can use them easier. This might include e.g. bigger icons, and less functionality. Senior *phones* finally denote phones specially designed to be simpler and exposing less functionality from the ground up.

As an example, the app *Oscar Senior*[1] is a senior app for smartphones and tablets, which should make the life of seniors easier. It offers a simple and friendly environment full of useful applications that help even complete beginners. Oscar offers a simple and well-arranged graphical interface with large elements and characters that are preferred by seniors. Additionally, the application is running in safe mode and blocks all pop-ups or notifications and allows the user to leave the application. Seniors will find everything they need on the Internet, from e-mails to useful applications such as medication reminders. Simplified communication enable seniors to make a video call with one click, or share photos or text messages to loved ones. The application can provide a course that teaches seniors, and can be used based on what is technically proficient.

BIG Launcher[2] is the first of its kind that has been developed for the elderly or for people who have certain vision problems. This launcher uses large buttons and large fonts to optimize work with smartphones running Android, to help seniors with problems reading smaller fonts and buttons.

Finally, there are several senior mobile phones, like BLU Tank 3 or Doro 410.[3] Such phones are usually simple, mainly for phone calls, with large physical buttons. As a special feature, some do have SOS buttons to send emergency SMSs to selected group of contacts.

To conclude, there have already been attempts to solve the problem addressed, each of the tools presented has its pros and cons. There are no definite solutions, only partial ones. Seniors should not be burdened by complicated functions, which will waste time and the risk that they will simply refuse to use smartphones anymore. Being a senior app, MuMail offers a simple design and users can see directly at first glance the purpose of each GUI element.

---

[1] https://play.google.com/store/apps/details?id=com.oscarsenior.oscar&hl=de.

[2] http://biglauncher.com/home/de/.

[3] http://www.makeuseof.com/tag/5-mobile-phones-senior-citizens/.

3 MuMail

Figure 1 shows a use-case diagram depicting how MuMail works. The app starts with a welcome page where the users can log in (Fig. 2). Before someone can use this app, the person must first have a valid email account. Many elderly people in western countries today have one, but are reluctant to use or manage them. Thus, this part of the setup might be done with the help of relatives or friends.

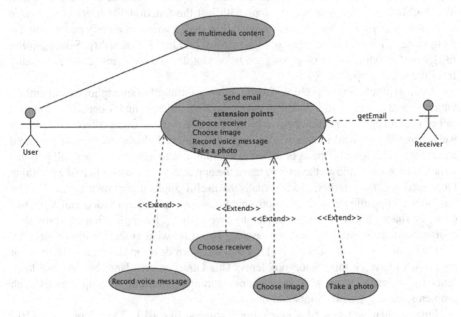

Fig. 1. MuMail use-case diagramm

Once the login is complete, the user can use the app immediately and use it in emergencies to ask for help. When the user logs in the next time, he will be forwarded to the Inbox page of MuMail without any further intermediate steps. This was also one of the main objectives of MuMail that design and operating the app is as simple as possible.

MuMail supports all major email providers, including Gmail, Hotmail, Outlook etc. As soon as the button "Done" is pressed, MuMail checkes whether all data has been entered correctly and if so, the user is redirected to the inbox page (Fig. 3).

Inbox

This is the most important page of the whole app. All the multimedia content is shown on this page. Users can browse through pictures, or play the voice messages. There is only one "Settings" button. Here the user can change his email account. With a simple swipe gesture the user can update his inbox and see, if there are any changes in the mailbox.

Fig. 2. MuMail login page

Fig. 3. MuMail inbox page

All the media content is saved in a sample UITableView, so with a simple swipe the user can browse between images and voice messages.

Sending Emails

MuMail is designed to work just with multimedia content like photos or video. However, users can send e-mails. First, a user can choose the recipient. To make it more convenient, users do not have to type a name, they just have a simple list with names and pictures, where they can choose the recipient with one tap. Then they have two options to choose from, they can either send an image or record a voice message. Users can choose images from the phone gallery or take a picture instantly. There is a limit for sending, i.e. a maximum of three images, to prevent seniors from sending too big emails. To send a voice message, there is a "record" icon. With the "play" icon users can hear, what they just recorded. Again, the design goal was to keep things simple and intuitive (Fig. 4).

Once the "Send email" button is clicked and an Internet connection is available, an indicator will be shown that the email was successfully sent.

Choose a recipient

To make choosing of a recipient easier, there is a list of favourite contacts, which can be edited by the user any time. User sees the email addresses and the pictures of their contacts, so seniors will not have to type a complicated email address by they own (Fig. 5).

To add a new contact, users simply press the "+" icon. Here they can type the email address and set the image for the contact. After pressing the "Done" button the contact

Fig. 4. MuMail send Email page

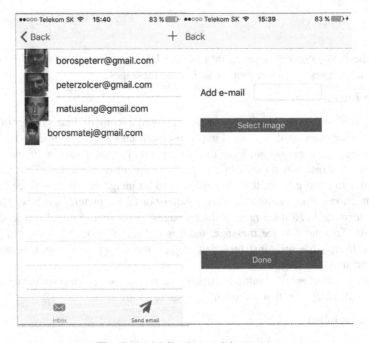

Fig. 5. MuMail select recipient page

will be added to the list and is ready to be chosen. If the user decides that he wants to delete a contact from the list, he can do it with a simple swipe, being a native iOS gesture.

4   Experimental Evaluation

After thorough technical evaluation using simulators and real iOS devices like iPhone 6S and iPad we tested the MuMail with an older person.

Our test person was a woman, 60 years old. She is still working and uses her email account. For testing she used an iPhone, but she does not own a smartphone herself. On this phone, MuMail was set to her email account. For doing this she actually did not need any help. After a successful login, voice messages and the images were shown in her Inbox immediately. She was very satisfied with swiping, seeing the pictures, hearing voice messages, there was no immediate problem that would stop her using the mail client.

Sending an email worked satisfactory as well. There is no button, which she could not understand or misuse in some way. She chose a contact from her favorite list, which had been configured for her. She was also able to add new contacts to this list by herself.

Likewise, attaching photos and sending them worked well with her, and she was able to send according emails without problems. In fact, the test person was so fond of MuMail that she is using it ever since.

5   Conclusion

Our goal was to connect seniors to their loved ones or their social peers by using a simple, multimedia oriented smartphone email client taking away unnecessary complexity. We have not seen such an app anywhere before. Instead, email clients and other multimedia apps in one way or the other are very difficult to be used by elderly people.

MuMail is an email client that delivers exactly this, simple audio/visual email for seniors based on standard email technology.

In the future we will continue to improve MuMail to include more functions without making the client more complicated. This includes e.g. audible notifications in case new emails were received. We will also include more languages in order to make MuMail internationally usable, especially in high-tech societies with a large senior population.

References

1. Apple: Objective C Documentation. Von Apple developer (2016). https://developer.apple. com/library/content/documentation/Cocoa/Conceptual/ProgrammingWithObjectiveC/ Introduction/Introduction.html
2. MailCore2: MailCore2 Documentation (2016). http://libmailcore.com/
3. OAuth2: OAuth2 Documentation (2016). https://oauth.net/2/
4. Mcmurtrey, M., Downey, J., Zeltmann, S., Mcgaughey, R.: Seniors and technology: results from a field study (2011)

Enabling Augmented Sense-Making (and Pure Experience) with Wearable Technology

Michel Witter[1(✉)] and Licia Calvi[2]

[1] Academy of Communication & User Experience, Expertise Centre for Art and Design EKV, Avans University of Applied Sciences, Breda, The Netherlands
mml.witter@avans.nl

[2] Academy for Digital Entertainment, NHTV Breda University of Applied Sciences, Breda, The Netherlands
calvi.l@nhtv.nl

Abstract. The paper explores how a post-cognitive approach to human perception can help the design of wearable technologies that augment sense-making. This approach relies on the notion of *pure experience* to understand how we can make sense of the world without interpreting it, for example through our body, as claimed by phenomenology. In order to understand how to design wearable technologies for pure experience, we first held interviews with experts from different domains, all investigating how to express and recognise pure experience. Subsequently, we had a focus group with professional dancers: given their heightened sense of bodily cognition in their experience, we wanted to verify the extent to which the experts' practice could be claimed back into the dancers' experience. In this paper, we will present our preliminary findings.

Keywords: Augmented sense-making · Embodied cognition
Wearable technology · Phenomenology · Dance · Pure experience

1 Introduction

Current wearable devices are mostly information appliances that are developed from a traditional cognitivist perspective that considers the computer user as an information processor [2]. Within this perspective, devices are seen as tools that mediate the experience through interaction with them.

Some scholars [4, 7] however express their concerns about this view because they claim that technology-as-a-tool mainly distracts users, who tend to focus more on the device itself than on the experience resulting from using it. When interacting with a technology allows users to experience the world without mediation, without interpretation, then such an interaction appears in its purest form: it is *pure experience*.

Several scholars refer to the role of the body in cognition and advocate for the need to design for the lived body and for being skilled in kinesthetic thinking and bodily intelligence [4, 7]. This seems particularly present in professional dancers [6]. Professional dancers indeed have developed something more than simple bodily or kinesthetic awareness: through their performance they "think feelingly" [5] and are aware of their perception that is influenced through action.

We claim that wearable technology can also help non-trained users develop this type of heightened embodied cognition and thus make way to achieve a state of pure experience, if this allows them to develop what we call *sense augmentation*. Subtle, intimate tactile qualities of interaction, which are hardly recognisable for bystanders or consciously unperceivable by the user concerned, can indeed have a significant effect on the value created while performing the interaction. Wearable technologies, by definition close to or on the body, do offer opportunities to explore these subtle, intimate qualities. In this paper, we precisely focus on the relation between augmented sense-making and movement, and its effect on a person's cognition.

This paper reports a preliminary study in which we explored how wearable devices that help users experience in this most basic and unspoiled way must be designed. This research is based on two approaches that are both a response to the information-processing and symbolic representation prevalent within cognitive sciences. The first is embodiment, a concept grounded in the phenomenology of Merleau-Ponty [8]. The second is enaction, which considers cognition as the result of a body in motion [11]. We will investigate how these approaches can be used in the design of artifacts that influence our perception at a phenomenological level. Our ultimate goal is to identify principles for the design of wearable technologies that heighten embodied cognition by providing new sensory stimuli that augment human perception. This augmented perception should such influence the sense-making process in order to reveal new pleasurable or surprising experiences.

In what follows, we will first give a clear definition of what pure experience is. In order to do so, we will have to explain also how pure experience relates to sense-making and enaction: we will discuss how sense-making is an important part of the enactive process of embodied interaction.

2 Why Pure Experience

Available interfaces, such as Kinect, Leap Motion, FitBit, and diverse mobile computing applications, enable the HCI community to explore embodied interaction, but they tend to create experiences that are designed from an instrumental viewpoint and ignore typical and personal bodily characteristics and knowledge from, e.g., embodied interaction. Information is presented in a way that distracts attention towards the experiences of others, ignoring the qualities of the individual's perception. We claim there is a need for attention for the individual user's interaction with the world and the subtle qualities hidden within the user experience as a result of that interaction. The intimate nature of wearable technology - intimate in that close to the body - offers opportunities for the technology to be transparent to the user and to provide unintended though meaningful experiences that go beyond those offered by more goal-directed, wearable, tools.

2.1 Pure Experience

The notion of pure experience is first introduced by James [1], who defines it as being "the immediate flux of life which furnishes the material to our later reflection". This highly philosophical interpretation of a pre-cognitive state tries to help imagine that human sense-making of the world starts with the phenomenological encounter with its surroundings. And that the sense-making process consists of successive small encounters, that are influenced by preceding ones and together build up knowledge. Hence through embodiment and a sensorimotor confrontation with the world, humans make sense of that world and the interactions presented in it. This is what enaction, based on the phenomenology of perception, instigated by Merleau-Ponty [8], is about. This knowledge is not yet understandable in a rationalist sense, though it is already cognition. This is exactly the focus of our research: a low-level cognitive experience that is hard to imagine for non-experts and that is difficult to measure using currently available research methods.

Pure experience provides, together with enaction, the initial theoretical backdrop needed for designing interactions that focus on the primal encounter between the user and her environment.

2.2 Sense-Making

An important part of meaning making is the "role of goal-directed bodily activity" ([3], p.1). In their study, Froese and colleagues discuss the design of interfaces that "serve as a transparent medium for augmenting our natural skills of interaction *with* the world, instead of requiring conscious attention to the interface as an opaque object *in* the world" ([3], p.1). This is also enaction.

As mentioned above, enaction claims the centrality of the body in cognition. It is the movement of the body as a response to a stimulus that creates meaning. Meaning is constructed through our interaction with the world, directly or via an artifact, where our senses transfer phenomena to our body, our body responds to these phenomena and meaning gets constructed through this reciprocal interaction.

This personal meaning-creation takes on a central role in this research. The goal of this study is precisely to help identify how to design artifacts that address our perception and cognition at the level of personal meaning-making through sensorimotor coupling. This should provide room for a more phenomenological level of perception. These newly designed technological products, if transparent to the user and not requiring conscious attention, promise to offer people the ability to perceive new phenomena, and consequently the possibility to develop a new, or augmented, sense of the world. We call this *augmented sense-making*.

3 Our Approach

We held a series of semi-structured in-depth interviews with experts, all focusing on the lived body but from different perspectives, in order to identify what elements or principles these expert professionals consider important when designing wearable technology from the perspective of pure experience in order to augment sense-making. Subsequently, we critically discussed the outcome of these interviews with a group of six professional dancers in a focus group session.

3.1 The Experts' Interviews

The interview experts are Marloeke van der Vlugt, a Dutch artist and researcher, Antal Ruhl, a lecturer in multimedia design, Tom Froese, associate professor and one of the researchers investigating the so-called enactive torch, and Pierre Lévy, assistant professor and expert into Kansei research. The interviews followed a predefined guide an interview guide and focused on topics such as intimate and wearable technology, pure experience, meaning and sense-making, senses and augmented sense-making.

Our experts seem to convene that:

- Pure experience can be considered as a naïve state of perception, something that is felt or lived and that can be expressed immediately without going through any rational thinking.
- Only trained people, like dancers, are able to recognise their phenomenological experience, because they have learned to express such experience physically in a more intuitive and immediate way than through thinking. Dancers are trained to be aware of their body and of their extensive sensory perception and to identify what sensory stimuli come from the outside world. They know how to communicate their individual phenomenological experience to the audience, through dance.

Our experts recognize two ways to augment sense-making: (1) enhancing what one can sense through the use of technology (as in [3]), or (2) improving one's sensory awareness through training, as dancers do. A nice example of a device that provides sensory augmentation related to a "forgotten" sense is the feelSpace belt [9] that constantly points at magnetic North by way of a built-in compass and vibration motors mounted on a belt around the waist. An in-depth systematic study of long-term use of this belt [9] shows how the spatial perception of the wearer is changed, even when she is not using the belt anymore.

3.2 The Focus Group

The focus group discussion took place in a room at the premises of dance company De Stilte in Breda. All six participants, aged 21 to 27, male and female, and the facilitator sat around a large table. Several questions were asked according to a focus group topic guide. The topics covered issues regarding the creation of meaning, perceiving "the invisible", the language of expression, and role of garments during performance and training. Due to technical issues, we could not carry out an experiment with the dancers wearing a specific wearable device. So, the participants' replies are mainly drawn from memory instead of from lived experiences.

Among other findings, the dancers turn out to possess an outstanding way to express their embodied interaction with each other and their environment. But, when it comes to expressing their phenomenological experience in specific situations verbally, even their vocabulary seems to be limited. As with non-trained people, during our conversation they were rationalising their felt experiences and started "thinking" about how they experienced it, instead of expressing directly what they had experienced. This is also a sign that the focus group was not the ideal method to understand lived experiences: the dancers had indeed difficulties understanding what we meant with our questions and could not always refer to the same phenomenon.

4 Preliminary Findings

Our preliminary findings, based on the insights gained through the expert interviews and the focus group session presented above, are that wearable technologies that augment sense-making should:

Support augmentation: wearable technology should augment, and not substitute, an existing sense, or trigger a supposedly latent sense that we unlearned through evolution, such as a sense of direction.

Be transparent: the interface of such wearable technology should be transparent to the user, non-intrusive, non-distracting. The focus is the primal experience they enhance, not their appearance or the social interaction they may facilitate.

Allow for sensorimotor integration: to emphasise how our bodily movements influence our ways of being and thinking, the body and our sensory appreciations should both play a central role in the design of wearable technology. As in [10], unconscious perception of touch and movement is important.

Facilitate an intimate experience: The body itself is the main interface for acquiring knowledge. Additionally, wearable technology should leave room for internal reflection on both external stimuli and personal phenomenological experiences.

Awake: wearable technology is designed to awaken pre-cognitive awareness.

5 Discussion and Next Steps

The findings reported in the previous section are based on a preliminary analysis of dancers' experience. It is debatable whether the focus on dancers is not too narrow and can potentially hinder understanding how untrained users could experience and perceive the world in this heightened way. Opening up the target group becomes a necessary next step. Moreover, we need to further extend empirical research on existing wearable technology to see whether our current findings can be mapped onto them.

In order to achieve this, we are setting up experiments bringing together trained dancers and interaction design students. Our goal is to capture pure experience data, through these experiments, for further analysis and to inspire design students through their encounter with dancers and the exchange of individual experiences. These experiments will be conducted using a selection of existing sense-augmenting devices, such as a compass belt similar to the feelSpace belt [9] mentioned earlier.

With the outcome of these experiments, we will design a concept for a sense-augmenting wearable device inspired by the notion of pure experience and complying with the principles just described.

6 Concluding Remarks

Our endeavor to design wearable technology from the perspective of pure experience is not an easy process. But, the enthusiastic responses of experts in the field of related domains, such as phenomenology and embodied interaction, and the genuine interest and valuable insights offered by the experts and dancers we interviewed did convince us that this is something worth doing. The dancers we contacted indicated their willingness to participate in further studies where they will try out any novel wearable device we might develop.

Acknowledgments. We wish to thank the dancers and artistic director Jack Timmermans of de Stilte, Tom Froese, Marloeke van der Vlugt, Pierre Lévy and Antal Ruhl.

References

1. Becker, H., James, W.: Essays in radical empiricism. Am. Sociol. Rev. **9**(5), 586 (1944)
2. Fällman, D.: In romance with the materials of mobile interaction: a phenomenological approach to the design of mobile information technology. Ph.D. thesis, Umeå University (2003)
3. Froese, T., McGann, M., Bigge, W., Spiers, A., Seth, A.K.: The enactive torch: a new tool for the science of perception. IEEE Trans. Haptics **5**(4), 365–375 (2012)
4. Höök, K., Ståhl, A., Jonsson, M., Mercurio, J., Karlsson, A., Banka, E.-C.: Somaesthetic design. Interactions **22**(4), 26–33 (2015)
5. Jacucci, G.: Interaction as Performance: Cases of Configuring Physical Interfaces in Mixed Media. Oulu University Press (2004)
6. Kirsh, D.: Embodied cognition and the magical future of interaction design. ACM Trans. Comput. Interact. **20**, 1–30 (2013)
7. Marti, P.: The subtle body. Inaugural lecture, TUE (2014)
8. Merleau-Ponty, M.: The Phenomenology of Perception (Smith, C., trans.). Humaniteit Press, New York (1962). (Original work published in 1945)
9. Nagel, S.K., Carl, C., Kringe, T., Märtin, R., König, P.: Beyond sensory substitution–learning the sixth sense. J. Neural Eng. **2**(4), R13–R26 (2005)
10. Schiphorst, T.: Really, really small. In: Proceedings of the 6th ACM SIGCHI Conference on Creativity & Cognition - C&C 2007, pp. 7–16 (2007)
11. Stewart, J., Gapenne, O., Di Paolo, E.A. (eds.): Enaction: Toward a New Paradigm for Cognitive Science. MIT Press, Cambridge (2010)

G:RASS – Experiencing a City Through an Artist's Eyes

Anastasia Treskunov[1], Christoph Vogel[1], Marta Wróblewska[2,3],
Michael Bertram[1], Fabian Büntig[1], and Christian Geiger[1(✉)]

[1] University of Applied Sciences Düsseldorf, Düsseldorf, Germany
geiger@hs-duesseldorf.de
[2] Gunter Grass Gallery, Gdańsk, Poland
[3] University of Gdańsk, Gdańsk, Poland

Abstract. We describe a mobile app that allows to enjoy a city experience through the artistic perspective of an artist. For the Gunter Grass Gallery in Gdańsk we designed and developed a user experience that presents work of Grass directly at the original locations. In his "Danzig Trilogy" the Nobel Prize winner Günter Grass described places of his hometown Danzig (now Gdańsk), how they used to be in the beginning of the 20th century. With the G:RASS-app the city gets surrounded by art pieces (text passages, drawings, sketches, audio). Using mixed reality, visitors can explore Gdańsk from the artist's point of view.

Keywords: Interactive city walks · Location-based mobile entertainment

1 Introduction

With the ongoing digitalization of cities and widespread use of mobile devices, the market for location-based services on smartphones is growing. Many available apps provide functionality for navigation, social interaction, entertainment and sightseeing. Few mobile applications provide a location-based access to art because there are few examples with a sound relation between art work and locations. We focus on the development of a mobile app for experience art fragments of the works of Günther Grass while walking through the inner city of Gdańsk, the native city of the artist. Aiming to motivate and empower people to explore their environments and discover the city of Gdańsk through the perspective of the artist should create a unique and entertaining experience. The project was initiated based on the insight that we often spend little time in our hectic daily life on mindfully experiencing our environments while maintaining a relation to artistic work with locations-based focus. Instead, we often commute from a start to an end-point in the most effective way and often use that time to work, read or simply kill time by engaging in social networking or playing mindless games on our smartphones. As a result, we are less aware of our surroundings and the exciting or beautiful things it might hold. The growth of digitization and the GPS-functions of mobile devices offer the possibilities to make cities playable and experience them in a whole different way. Also, it is possible to shape the city towards a given artistic experience without changing it in real life. Our aim was to represent Grass' work in a playful, entertaining and unusual way.

© ICST Institute for Computer Sciences, Social Informatics and Telecommunications Engineering 2018
Y. Chisik et al. (Eds.): INTETAIN 2017, LNICST 215, pp. 142–145, 2018.
https://doi.org/10.1007/978-3-319-73062-2_12

Similar projects differ in the way they present artistic content. The app "Flaneur" [1] developed for the public library in Düsseldorf uses cutouts from literature, films and music and brings them to bizarre places of the city. The quotations, film parts or songs are chosen to underline the peculiarity of a certain place. The aim of this app is to bring back the serendipity of using digital libraries by offering media elements depending on the user' location. "A secret golden age" [2] is a mobile app project by the University of Edinburgh, which is made for long-term Edinburgh residents and first-time visitors. After choosing one of five available routes, the mobile application leads you through the city of Edinburgh. On specific spots the application provides recent literary research and historical information as well as literary extracts along the way. The application focuses on literature written in English and Latin. Furthermore there is a project from the University of Iowa, "The city of Lit", that also exploits the user's location for a literary experience. Examples of geo-tagged events include locations of local readings, former dwellings of resident writers, and fictional or real Iowa City locations referenced in literature. Based on this, the user can take a literary stroll through the Iowa City [3]. The Bux app makes it possible to discover Zurich from eleven different authors' points of view. They guide you to the certain places to get the quotations and for example pose virtual with you for a photo. For this app, the Zurich University of Arts, the Commission for Technology and Innovation and different publishing companies worked together [4]. The technical concept of our app was also based on STOYL, a location-based approach to music listening with a serendipity-based approach to experience the music library of other users [5].

2 Concept and Implementation

G:RASS [Gdańsk: real and simulated spaces] leads the user along the route of motifs taken from Grass's books. This project is based on digital media and mixed reality technologies, implemented thanks to the collaboration between the Gallery and the University of Applied Sciences Düsseldorf, in result of the partnership within the Creative Europe project – The People's Smart Sculpture. The authors of the script are Piotr Wyrzykowski, a visual artist familiar with mixed reality projects and the poet Andrzej Fac. The main idea of the app is going out into the public space (both virtually and physically) to rediscover it through the oeuvre of Günter Grass. Prinz – the dog from the novel "Dog years/Hundejahre" (one of the three novels of the so-called Gdańsk trilogy) becomes the city guide, taking the users on a walk through Gdańsk and leading them to selected places full of different surprising pieces of information and sensations. One of the main goals of this project is its accessibility – physical, cultural and financial. That is why the app is free of charge, and its content is friendly to all kinds of users regardless of age or education. It has been prepared not only for the inhabitants of Gdańsk, but also with a view to the foreign visitors – hence it can be used in three languages: Polish, German and English. Günter Grass was a very distinctive person. He is famous as a writer, but was also sculptor and painter. Aim was to filter all his work and convey it in a multimedia way by connecting it with the real surroundings. Here it was very helpful to have a Günter-Grass-expert joining our team, who knows about his complex work and the person. Our first step was to work through

Grass' "Danzig Trilogy" where he describes several places in Gdansk. The novel "Dog Years" was the main inspiration for this project and based on this, we selected eleven locations in the city. Aim was to develop a tour that takes about an hour. Also, using a dog as guide that leaves a trail where to go next was a good way to illustrate selected perceptions. When a quotation was talking about the smell of fire, an illustration of a sniffing dog augments the quote (Fig. 1).

Fig. 1. Interface and design elements from the G:RASS mobile app

Every station is designed in a special way using illustrations, photos, quotations and sound recordings. The illustrations are inspired by the drawings of Günter Grass, which are presented in the gallery. During the project, we received significant help from institutions based in Gdansk. For example, when we needed recordings from a choir, we collaborated with the main choir of the city. At the amber market, we placed photos of an amber sculpture made by a contemporary local artist. Initial tests showed that the usability is easy and self-explaining by using mostly symbols (Fig. 2).

Fig. 2. Interface and design elements from the G:RASS mobile app

The G:RASS application was developed as a mobile app for the Android operating system. The system was implemented with the Unity3D version 5.4 game engine, because it provides easy integration for multiple deployment platforms and fast prototyping possibilities. Due to the limited possibility of continual presence at the location the use of Unity3D also facilitated the remote testing and development directly on Windows computer. Marker-based AR tracking was not possible in this case because of the changing light situation during its outdoor use. Instead, we used a GPS-location based positioning approach to approximate the world position of the device. At key locations in Gdansk the content aligns according to the cardinal directions using the plugin GyroDroid for sensor fusion.

3   Conclusion

Valuable information for future improvements of the app was collected in a workshop with students from Gdansk. Around 20 students aged from 16 to 19 years participated in the workshop. After a short introduction of the content and functions of the application, the students offered suggestions for its additional features and further enhancements. The following remarks originated from the workshop: 'The app should contain a lot of interesting functions', '...be safe for the user', '...contain translations in various languages', '...take little memory space', '...contain colourful characters and interesting plot', '...be accessible to everyone', '...give opportunity to create your own avatar', '...contain elaborate graphics', '...have an option of guide selection', '...have an option to choose a short or a longer route', '...contain short information about the places', '...be accessible to a greater number of devices'.

This paper described the design and development of G:RASS, a mixed reality app, that shows Gdańsk from Grass' point of view. The application shows that his work isn't bound to the medium of a book and can be integrated in a mobile app using different media. Therefore, it can be easier available for young users, tourists or people who want to discover his work in another way. The work shows that the mixed reality function offers an interesting way to present artistic information in real city spaces. This opens new opportunities to access literature for new user groups.

Acknowledgments.   This work was partially supported by the Polish-German Cooperation Foundation and Creative Europe EU Program (The People's Smart Sculpture).

References

1. Treskunov, A.: Flaneur – Master thesis, University of Applied Sciences Düsseldorf (2016)
2. A secret golden age. www.asecretgoldenage.com/about-the-project/
3. Draxler, B., Hsieh, H., Dudley, N., Winet, J.: City of Lit: collaborative research in literature and new media. J. Interact. Technol. Pedagogy (1) (2012). https://goo.gl/tVKAlM
4. Discover Literature in Zurich with the new Bux App. www.bux-app.ch/
5. Huldtgren, A., Mayer, C., Kierepka, O., Geiger, C.: Towards serendipitous urban encounters with SoundtrackOfYourLife. In: Proceedings of the 11th Conference on Advances in Computer Entertainment Technology (ACE 2014). ACM, New York (2014)

Placemaking Across Platforms: Playing to Circulate Stories in the Smart City

Benjamin Stokes[1(✉)], Karl Baumann[2], and François Bar[3]

[1] School of Communication, American University,
4400 Massachusetts Ave NW, Washington, D.C. 20016, USA
bstokes@american.edu
[2] Schools of Cinematic Arts and Communication, University of Southern California, 3470 McClintock Ave, Los Angeles, CA 90089, USA
kbaumann@usc.edu
[3] School of Communication, University of Southern California,
3502 Watt Way, Los Angeles, CA 90089, USA
fbar@usc.edu

Abstract. Urban placemaking can deepen the sense of place, including with novel technologies. Placemaking seeks to revitalize public spaces, attract investment, and rally stakeholders. How can play help to position residents as storytellers and circulators of key images tied to local history? This study shows how play can leverage smart city technologies, including urban furniture and rebuilt payphones. Game mechanics were selected to gather crowds at local monuments, generate pictures of the group tied to local mythology, and automatically circulate images online. In contrast to "app" based approaches, the design facilitated cross-platform "spread" for local storytelling. The study shows how placemaking can benefit from physical objects and hybrid interfaces to facilitate the circulation of local placemaking narratives.

Keywords: Playful · Smart city · Tangible object · Placemaking · Stories

1 Introduction

The movement for "creative placemaking" offers a growing opportunity for games in smart cities and neighborhoods. Placemaking seeks to revitalize public spaces and bring together local actors to shape the character and experience of a neighborhood.

Recent shifts in placemaking have made pervasive games [1] especially relevant. The placemaking movement has expanded beyond branding and architecture to include *creative activities* that deepen our sense of place and attachment to it [2]. Games offer a powerful way to design such activities, especially as our places become hybrids of physical space and digital information flows [3].

Smart cities have a growing range of basic technologies available to facilitate placemaking, from screens embedded in public space [4] to mobile media [5] that move with residents. Beyond sharing information, technologies can facilitate social activity and transform how we experience a place [6]. Play can further deepen our sense of place, even functioning as a form of urban planning [7]. Structured games can leverage smart city technology, for example by co-opting existing urban screens as part of

© ICST Institute for Computer Sciences, Social Informatics and Telecommunications Engineering 2018
Y. Chisik et al. (Eds.): INTETAIN 2017, LNICST 215, pp. 146–150, 2018.
https://doi.org/10.1007/978-3-319-73062-2_13

festivals [8], and reaching consumers in the "app economy" with locative games [9]. But how can games position players as active placemakers themselves?

A novel strategy for games is to facilitate the *circulation* of placemaking stories and images. Circulation is necessary for citizens to discover local stories from each other, spread the stories they care about, and bring historical facts into lived culture. Content for circulation includes the photographs of iconic buildings, tales of local history, and testimony about cultural assets. Games can position players as direct circulators of multimedia, and as live performers drawing attention to public space.

To maximize circulation across platforms, this study advances two design strategies. First, for games in smart cities this study explores the use of *smart tangible objects* to connect the circulation of bodies and digital media. Such objects facilitate street-level storytelling, while also serving as hybrid interfaces [10] to guide players through space, providing clues and feedback. Second, rather than focusing player attention inward to game content, this paper investigates content as *spreadable media* [11] that is optimized for players to circulate across their personal networks, including with web links that can easily be shared or reposted.

2 Game Design and User Trials

A game prototype called *Sankofa Says* was developed for a small California city that was already pursuing placemaking. The game took place over a weekend in a 10-block area, during a game festival that brought many visitors to town for the first time. Content was developed in consultation with the local historical society.

Playing involved gathering crowds at local monuments, performing as historic characters, taking cellphone pictures, and calling a cloud-based hotline for group trivia questions about the neighborhood. The technical design connected multiple platforms, including cloud-based audio hotlines, picture messaging, and smart tangible objects (e.g., a rebuilt payphone containing a Raspberry Pi computer [12]).

Players gained points by gathering in crowds at historic landmarks and key sites. Team members earned additional points based on the size of the group, encouraging recruiting. Parades formed as groups walked between landmarks, sometimes spontaneously and sometimes led by game facilitators with megaphones.

At each landmark, players used their cellphones to dial a smart hotline. The hotline recognized each player using caller ID, and gave them information on the current crowd. New players could sign up by phone to join the crowd at any time. After players' individual calls, the crowd staged a group photograph at the landmark (e.g., the site of a famous battle – see Fig. 1).

When the crowd submitted a photograph (using the phone of any one participant), the game system reposted it automatically to a blog for that landmark. The result was a public narrative of what happened at that landmark, including pictures and a record of players who joined the crowd (using their first name or pseudonym of choice). Later, the best pictures for each landmark were moved to the top of the page.

A rebuilt portable payphone served as an object to spark curiosity – and as a recruiting station. The payphone included a loudspeaker system that was used to announce special events at landmarks (Fig. 2). For example, players might be told of a special guest arriving at a nearby landmark in 15 min.

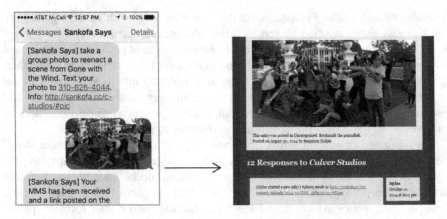

Fig. 1. Screenshots of player phone during game, and resulting webpage

Fig. 2. Rebuilt payphone as tangible object *(left)*; social and paper media *(right)*

When players lifted the handset, the rebuilt payphone played audio that invited them to learn more. "Press 1 to play," and "Press 4 for more on the city" were two of the options. Many were curious about the payphone itself.

Local, pre-existing payphones were also incorporated into the game route. Two of the landmarks featured working payphones in the city that required quarters to play. One served as the gathering spot for what local news outlets have proudly insisted is the "World's Smallest Main Street," next to an antique store.

Mixing old payphones with the history of the city helped embody the idea of living history. Placemaking often relies on historic assets that can be repositioned to tell a story of local distinction, creating in the process a new vision for where the community will go in the future. Payphones are ideal for stories about urban futures, as they embody a blending of physical and communication infrastructures [12].

After the game, news websites and local blogs covering *Sankofa Says* told their own stories of the city. Additionally, a planning meeting for the city's Centennial

Celebration included a review of pictures taken of the game, leading to a discussion with the Chamber of Commerce about how to continue the placemaking.

In total, more than 30 players directly engaged with the game, and several hundred observers and peers were involved in the story circulation. The game's structural role was then analyzed through more than a dozen participant interviews, "post-mortem" sessions with notes, and interviews with stakeholders (e.g., the local historical society). Beyond individual effects, the game shifted the circulation of placemaking stories during its trial run – both in person and online.

3 Discussion and Conclusions

This case investigated the use of games for placemaking in smart cities and communities. In contrast to the tradition of secrecy and conspiracy of Alternate Reality Games in public space [13], placemaking seeks publicity, transparency and building trust around the core narratives. This study advances how games can facilitate the circulation of stories, including through designs that make players visible in the city, center competition on gathering crowds, encourage taking pictures at iconic sites, and automate the reposting of key photographs online.

Design choices for game infrastructure can help to position players as active circulators of stories, and thus as placemakers. For smart cities, one strategy is to combine smart tangible objects (including urban furniture like rebuilt payphones) [14] with traditional print media for gameplay [15]. Other urban furniture that might be similarly deployed includes bus stops, newspaper boxes, and even smart benches (as the authors have done in other interventions [16]). Avoiding the "app economy" of mobile phones can also increase accessibility by reducing the need for downloads.

Authenticity and accountability to the community are central to placemaking concerns, including the process of choosing which landmarks to emphasize. Authority shifts when games empower players, and this study revealed some of the fault lines – and strategies to manage them. Working with historians and community organizations can help inoculate designs to the risk of excessive deferral to business visions of neighborhoods [17], and the shallow notions of culture that can arise in place-branding. But there remain uncertainties in play (and in fact, uncertainty is a defining characteristic of games [18]). In *Sankofa Says*, historians were consulted on the recommendation of organizations with broader stakes in the community. Yet the game encouraged visitors who were new to the neighborhood to take pictures and circulate local knowledge in their own words. Risks come with such openness, even as participation is guided by the structures and seed content of the game.

In an age of hybrid interfaces, new tactics are needed for creative placemaking. As this study showed, games are one way to advance placemaking by spreading digital stories tied to physical experiences and crowds. To be effective at circulating stories, games may need to encourage crossing platforms rather than using a single app, object, or form of media. Yet the ethics and permissions of play raise distinct challenges. It will be up to communities to invest in games as a placemaking strategy.

References

1. Montola, M., Stenros, J., Waern, A.: Pervasive Games: Theory and Design. Morgan Kaufmann, Burlington (2009)
2. Markusen, A., Gadwa, A.: Creative Placemaking. National Endowment for the Arts, Washington, D.C. (2010)
3. Gordon, E., de Souza e Silva, A.: Net Locality: Why Location Matters in a Networked World. Wiley-Blackwell, Hoboken (2011)
4. Wouters, N., Claes, S., Moere, A.V.: Investigating the role of situated public displays and hyperlocal content on place-making. IxD&A **25**, 60–72 (2015)
5. de Souza e Silva, A., Sheller, M.: Mobility and Locative Media: Mobile Communication in Hybrid Spaces. Routledge, Florence (2014)
6. Fatah gen Schieck, A.: Towards an integrated architectural media space: the urban screen as a socialising platform. In: McQuire, S., Martin, M., Niederer, S. (eds.) Urban Screens Reader, pp. 243–260. Institute of Network Cultures, Amsterdam (2009)
7. Innocent, T.: Play and placemaking in urban art environments. In: Proceedings of the 3rd Conference on Media Architecture Biennale, pp. 2:1–2:4. ACM, New York (2016)
8. Gullick, D., Burnett, D., Coulton, P.: Visual abstraction for games on large public displays. In: Poppe, R., Meyer, J.-J., Veltkamp, R., Dastani, M. (eds.) INTETAIN 2016. LNICST, vol. 178, pp. 271–275. Springer, Cham (2017). https://doi.org/10.1007/978-3-319-49616-0_27
9. Leorke, D.: Location-based gaming apps and the commercialization of locative media. In: de Souza e Silva, A., Sheller, M. (eds.) Mobility and Locative Media: Mobile Communication in Hybrid Spaces, pp. 132–148. Routledge, Florence (2014)
10. de Souza e Silva, A.: From cyber to hybrid mobile technologies as interfaces of hybrid spaces. Space Cult. **9**, 261–278 (2006)
11. Jenkins, H., Ford, S., Green, J.: Spreadable Media: Creating Value and Meaning in a Networked Culture. New York University Press, New York (2012)
12. Stokes, B., Baumann, K., Caldwell, B., Bar, F.: Neighborhood planning of technology: physical meets digital city from the bottom-up with aging payphones. J. Community Inform. **10** (2014)
13. Mcgonigal, J.: This is not a game: immersive aesthetics and collective play. In: Melbourne DAC 2003 Streamingworlds Conference Proceedings. RMIT University (2003)
14. Rubegni, E., Brunk, J., Caporali, M., Gronvall, E., Alessandrini, A., Rizzo, A.: Wi-Wave: urban furniture for browsing internet contents in public spaces. In: Proceedings of the 15th European Conference on Cognitive Ergonomics: The Ergonomics of Cool Interaction. pp. 10:1–10:7. ACM, New York (2008)
15. Taylor, M., Whatley, A.: Macon Money Final Evaluation Report. Knight Foundation, Miami (2012)
16. Baumann, K., Stokes, B., Bar, F., Caldwell, B.: Designing in "constellations": sustaining participatory design for neighborhoods. In: Proceedings of the 14th Participatory Design Conference: Short Papers, Interactive Exhibitions, Workshops, pp. 5–8. ACM Press, Aarhus (2016)
17. Ashworth, G.J., Kavaratzis, M.: Rethinking the roles of culture in place branding. In: Kavaratzis, M., Warnaby, G., Ashworth, G.J. (eds.) Rethinking Place Branding, pp. 119–134. Springer, Cham (2015). https://doi.org/10.1007/978-3-319-12424-7_9
18. Salen, K., Zimmerman, E.: Rules of Play: Game Design Fundamentals. MIT Press, Cambridge (2004)

Smart Magic City Run: Exploring the Implications of Public Augmented Reality Games

Daniel Pargman[✉], Tina Ringenson, Miriam Börjesson Rivera,
Lisa Schmitz, Maria Krinaki, Nino Prekratic, and Björn Lundkvist

KTH Royal Institute of Technology, 100 44 Stockholm, Sweden
{pargman, krin, miriamrg, lschmitz,
krinaki, ninop, blundk}@kth.se

Abstract. This paper presents an augmented reality smart city gaming concept, Magic Run. Magic Run has entertainment value and fulfills its' original brief, but several aspects of the game were found to be problematic during a workshop with smart city researchers. We present problematic aspects of the game as well as ideas for how to redesign the game to control or ameliorate problematic interaction between future smart city players and bystanders.

Keywords: Augmented reality · Smart city · Pervasive games
Speculative design · Design fiction

1 Introduction

With smart city initiatives popping up left, right and center, questions that have confounded city planners and social scientist for centuries once more inscribe themselves in the physical environs and at the top of our agendas; who and what is the city for? According to a definition from the Centre of Regional Science at Vienna University, "smart cities" are characterized by (1) smart economy, (2) smart people (3) smart governance, (4) smart mobility, (5) smart environment and (6) smart living [8]. Many visions and definitions of smart cities firmly focus on information technologies that optimize resource flows of various kinds (food, people, traffic, decisions etc.) in a top-down manner, and it has been suggested that such visions are compatible with authritarian agendas [9]. What can be unequivocally stated is that many visions, by almost exclusively focusing on *technologies*, become bloodless and lack ideas or suggestions about how *humans* will live their everyday lives and partake in various social practices [16] in the smart cities of the future [4]. So is the future smart city primarily an efficient machine for transporting goods and people hither and dither or is it also a space for spontaneity, interaction, leisure and free play?

We assume the latter and here describe a student project that resulted in a concept for a pervasive augmented reality game, Magic Run[1]. The game concept has since been

---

[1] For more information about Magic Run, see the powerpoint presentation, the book chapter and the short concept movie at http://fom.csc.kth.se/archive/.

© ICST Institute for Computer Sciences, Social Informatics and Telecommunications Engineering 2018
Y. Chisik et al. (Eds.): INTETAIN 2017, LNICST 215, pp. 151–158, 2018.
https://doi.org/10.1007/978-3-319-73062-2_14

"leveled up" by running it through smart city researchers who have scrutinized and noticed various troubling elements of the proposed game. We have then together redesigned the game by suggesting various improvements and suggestions for how the gaming concept (Magic Run 2.0) could be redesigned to better fit the reality of the smart future city.

Magic Run is a design fiction scenario [3, 7] that we believe could be realized 5–15 years from now; shorter if we assume Google glasses or goggles and later if we insist on digital contact lenses as the display technology of choice. The main challenge that Magic Run attempted to solve (or ameliorate) was an imagined future where an army of well-entertained couch potatoes did not get enough exercise [15]. Magic Run was our proposal for getting people outdoors, getting people to run and getting people to interact in and with public spaces.

2   Magic Run

After a long day at work you leave the office to go for your daily run and head to the nearby park. As you enter the park, butterflies appear around you and fluffy, friendly clouds cover the sky. It's time to warm up! Bright yellow stars start to appear over your head and you jump up and down trying to catch as many as you can in one single minute. After that minute has passed, your score shows +500 - a new highscore! Accompanied by the magical butterflies you let your pulse calm down while you run at a comfortable pace. But you shouldn't get too comfortable with that pace because now it's time for a sprint. A Magic Run colibri appears out of nowhere, flutters teasingly in front of you and then shoots ahead. You speed up and try to follow the colorful bird. As you catch up and your hand touches the colibri it disappears in a cloud of sparkles that earns you another +500 points.

This concept, Magic Run, has been developed to motivate people to exercise outdoors, transforming an activity that some might consider boring into a game, thereby tapping into additional sources of motivation. The original source of inspiration was the game "Zombie, Run![2]" as well as the immense success of the location-based mobile game Pokémon GO (it was downloaded more than 500 million times in the eight weeks following its release[3]). The Magic Run prototype combines the fun game mechanics of popular platform games (e.g. Nintendo's Mario games) with outdoors exercise. The user becomes the main character of the Magic Run game and the real world becomes a game world that the user interacts with through the movements of her own body. While the jury is out as to the sustained effects of gamification efforts in relation to medium- or long-term behavior change [10], we also note the huge popularity of apps that track and support exercise and fitness in the form of walking, running and cycling. The most popular app, RunKeeper[4], has 50 million users and we therefore assume there will be a market for a well-designed augmented reality app in that space.

---

[2] Six to Start and Naomi Alderman, 2012. See further https://zombiesrungame.com.

[3] See http://pokemongo.nianticlabs.com/en/post/headsup.

[4] FitnessKeeper, 2008. See further https://runkeeper.com.

The user can interact with Magic Run game objects in various ways, enabling different types of exercise. Collectables like stars are located above the user's head, encouraging her to jump, and catching a fast magical bird gives a concrete purpose to sprint intervals. These minigames bring more playfulness to the daily run, helping the user improve her physical fitness and overall health. It is possible to play Magic Run alone or together with others (cooperating or competing).

To implement Magic Run, we expect future augmented reality glasses or goggles that can augment the real environment with digital content. Combined with GPS technology and a depth sensor, it ought to be possible to play Magic Run in the near future. While designing the game, weaknesses and deficiencies of available technologies should be kept in mind. Hovering objects like butterflies and clouds are easier to blend into the environment than a tree that grows from the ground up, and a colibri (floating in mid-air) is preferable to rendering a rabbit running on the ground (which was part of the original game concept). Smart design of the game world can thus help obscure flaws and alleviate weaknesses of the current state of the art of augmented reality technologies.

3 Augmented Reality Game Challenges

The success of Pokémon GO[5] has led to many questions about health and safety. While the game does get people out and moving, including parents playing together with their children [17], there have also been reports of people engaging in problematic or dangerous behaviours, for example trespassing, suboptimal parking or risky driving [12]. There is also parental concerns about safety in real-world environments [17], not the least due to examples of a blatant lack of normal risk assessment; four teenagers had to be rescued from a vast mining complex where they had gone to catch Pokémons [5] and two men in the US accidentally fell off a cliff while playing [11]. An informant in the study by Sobel et al. [17] pointedly said *"I don't want my kids to be the dumb dumbs who fall of a cliff or [get] run over by a car because they [are] too engaged."* Media reports of dangers often emphasize straying into the wrong *places*, but the more widespread risk is that of *movement* in combination with reduced environmental awareness of road traffic [6]. This ties back to early examples of mobile gamers *"colliding with strangers when playing"* [2], but, if this happens while *walking*, what then are the possible consequences of playing while *running*? The faster speed and the shorter time to react to dangers together with the excitement of the gameplay and a lack of attention to the surrounding non-virtual environment could be a toxic cocktail. These dangers are an *intrinsic* part of the game and they represent problems the original Magic Run game design did not consider.

Beyond these direct risks, it is also possible to imagine that various forms of "non-conformist" behaviour could elicit negative reactions from bystanders. In a text that received much attention, Akil [1] discussed risks for black American men to play Pokémon GO in light of the possibility that (a) someone calls the police because a

---

[5] Niantic, 2016. See further: https://support.pokemongo.nianticlabs.com.

black man is exhibiting unusual or inexplicable behaviors and (b) some policemen might be prone to use powerful means to "control" the situation, up to and including employing potentially deadly gunfire. If mere existence in public spaces (being at the wrong place at the wrong time) can put black American men in harm's way, what then about someone inexplicably jumping, running, panting, shouting or suddenly changing direction and running *towards you*? The risk that such behaviors could frighten people in public spaces and elicit potentially dangerous reactions seems quite high (especially in societies where gun ownership is widespread). The disproportional distribution of such risks between social and racial groups points at the need for broader change in society. Still, the risk that all groups and all types of players can be misunderstood and perceived as behaving in dangerous ways is something that to the highest extent possible should be mitigated by redesigning the game.

It should be noted that some researchers have pointed out that most pervasive, location-based and mixed reality games are designed to provide players with limited experiences, e.g. *"The majority take the form of treasure hunts, where players must visit real-world locations in order to tick off game-world tasks"* [14]. While the call for games that provoke, that cause *"anxiety and exhileration"* and that are designed to be *"in opposition with, or disruptive of, social rules of the environment in which they are played"* [14, see also 13] is extremely intriguing, we deem it less suitable in this particular context as we potentially are dealing with people's health and safety.

4 Redesign and Outcome

If Magic Run and similar games potentially endanger the lives of its users, we urgently need to discuss possible changes in the design of the game. We will briefly discuss three avenues of thought to that effect, the first being aimed at increasing the security of bystanders, the second at increasing the safety of players and the third discussing emergent norms that mediate between bystanders and players.

Bystanders. It is crucial to redesign Magic Run in such a way that it does not become a public disturbance, for example by avoiding rewarding or encouraging behavior that could lead to annoyance or anxiety in bystanders. Jumping up and down in the same place (catching stars while warming up) might be ok but making giant leaps over imaginary obstacles less so. Using a large stone or a bench as a stepping stone to jump and reach higher could be a borderline case. It is an open question whether the game, using microphones, should penalize shouts and other outbursts that could worry bystanders, even though it would be thought provoking to for example encourage players to shout simultaneously (also enabling them to identify each other). The implications for public safety, anxiety and annoyance unfortunately highlights an innate tension with some of the core pleasures of playing the game (i.e. jumping up in the air to catch an imaginary star, see further Fig. 1 below). It might be possible to map game content to physical aspects of reality by aligning the placement of stars that can be caught just below trees with low-hanging branches. It would not look particularly strange to jump at such a place in comparison to jumping as high as you can "in the middle of nowhere".

Fig. 1. In the same way Mario jumps to catch stars and prizes in classic platform games, so could you become the hero of your own game by combining gameplay with moderate or vigorous exercise.

Players. The safety of players is very important as aspects of physical reality - dangerous terrain and especially traffic – could constitute risks for players. One possible solution is to restrict the game in space, making sure that it is only possible to play Magic Run in geofenced "safe" areas (for example in parks or designated forest or jogging trails). This opens up questions of how such spaces should be selected and by whom? We suggest a tight integration with data from geographic information systems (GIS) to find suitable areas. Such top-down data can however be incorrect or out of date and we would also suggest bottom-up approaches. Assuming that runners in general tend to seek out areas that are suitable for running in terms of safety and comfort, a running app such as Runkeeper could be mined for data about suitable locations and tracks in much the same way that Niantic used the database from their previous location-based game, Ingress, in the design of Pokémon GO.

Emergent player-bystander norms. Just as bystanders now understand that people seemingly talking to themselves most probably are talking in a mobile headset, we here assume that norms and practices around an augmented reality game like Magic Run would change over time. It could for example be the case that players prefer to use tight-fitting goggles rather than glasses and that such goggles will become the equivalent of a headset - signaling that the player is partially enclosed in a virtual world. This would furthermore seem particularly probable if the player is dressed in a tracksuit. Playing only in certain (geofenced) areas would also make it easier for both players and bystanders to successfully negotiate the use of public spaces despite the fact that there again is a basic tension between the sheer annoyance of bystanders minding their own business (strolling, having a picnic etc.) in relation to the chance that a player becomes absorbed in the gameplay to the detriment of other people's use of public space.

Space does not allow us to elaborate on these and other suggestion here but for one last idea. If augmented reality glasses become popular, it would be possible to imagine that bystanders are allowed a limited shared augmented reality view, for example in the shape of visible slipstream (glitter dust or some other customisable visual effect) that would follow Magic Run players and that would help bystanders understand players' mildly unorthodox behavior in public spaces.

5 Future Research

While we have concentrated on a limited number of issues in this short paper, e.g. on increasing the security of bystanders (by not freightening or annoying them) and on increasing the safety of players, it is possible to discern specific themes in the paper that we suggest should be addressed by future research. We need more research on:

- Social and power-related issues in relation to the unequal risk of becoming the object of suspicion by others.
- Evolving signaling strategies and the negotiation of acceptable behavior in the nexus of (novel) technologies and social practices in public spaces.
- The creation of more site-specific experiences through the sourcing of geo-data about features of the urban environment and bottom-up data about (in this case) runners' preferred routes.
- How to protect players from road traffic and other unsafe situation by manually or automatically geo-fencing suitable tracks or spaces for players.

6 Discussion

We have here presented a concept of a smart city pervasive augmented reality game, Magic Run. We have also discussed possible complications when the game is played in public spaces in the future smart city as well as some suggestions for ways to ameliorate said problems. Visionary Xerox PARC researcher Alan Kay said almost 50 years ago that "*the best way to predict the future is to invent it*". While Kay and his collaborators at Xerox PARC literally built parts of the future we now live in from the hardware and up, we have instead designed the future through the use of a speculative design scenario [3, 7]. By doing so we hope to open up the space for debate, discussions and social dreaming [7] about the future smart city to broader groups of participants than just engineers and software developers – because the city belongs to everyone who lives there!

Acknowledgements. We wish to thank the two anonymous reviewers for helpful comments and we especially want to thank the reviewer whose suggests became the backbone of the Future Research section of the paper.

References

1. Akil, O.: Warning: Pokemon GO is a death sentence if you are a black man. Mob. Lifestyle (2016). https://medium.com/mobile-lifestyle/warning-pokemon-go-is-a-death-sentence-if-you-are-a-black-man-acacb4bdae7f
2. Bell, M., Chalmers, M., Barkhuus, L., Hall, M., Sherwood, S., Tennent, P., Brown, B., Rowland, D., Benford, S., Capra, M., Hampshire, A.: Interweaving mobile games with everyday life. In: Proceedings of the SIGCHI Conference on Human Factors in Computing Systems, pp. 417–426. ACM, April 2006
3. Bleecker, J.: Design fiction. A short essay on design, science, fact and fiction. Near Future Laboratory (2009)
4. Börjesson Rivera, M., Eriksson, E., Wangel, J.: ICT practices in smart sustainable cities: in the intersection of technological solutions and practices of everyday life. In: Proceedings of EnviroInfo & ICT for Sustainability, pp. 317–324. Atlantis Press (2015). http://dx.doi.org/10.2991/ict4s-env-15.2015.36
5. Chandler, M.: Pokémon GO: four teens get lost in mine complex for five hours after hunting Pokémon. Evening Standard, 15 July 2016. http://www.standard.co.uk/news/techandgadgets/pok-mon-go-four-teens-get-lost-in-mine-complex-for-five-hours-after-hunting-pok-mon-a32 97261.html
6. Colley, A., Thebault-Spieker, J., Lin, A.Y., Degraen, D., Fischman, B., Häkkilä, J., Kuehl, K., Nisi, V., Nunes, N.J., Wenig, N., Wenig, D., Hecht, B., Schöning, J.: The geography of Pokémon GO: beneficial and problematic effects on places and movement. In: Proceedings of CHI 2017, pp. 1179–1192. ACM (2017)
7. Dunne, A., Raby, F.: Speculative Everything: Design, Fiction, and Social Dreaming. MIT Press, Cambridge (2013)
8. Giffinger, R., Fertner, C., Kramar, H., Kalasek, R., Pichler-Milanovic, N., Meijers, E.: Smart cities. Ranking of European medium-sized cities, Final Report, Centre of Regional Science, Vienna, UT (2007)
9. Greenfield, A.: Against the Smart City. Do Projects, New York City (2013)
10. Hamari, J., Koivisto, J., Sarsa, H.: Does gamification work?–A literature review of empirical studies on gamification. In: 2014 47th Hawaii International Conference on System Sciences (HICSS), pp. 3025–3034. IEEE (2014)
11. Hernanez, D.: 'Pokemon Go' players fall off 90-foot ocean bluff. The San Diego Union-Tribune, 13 July 2016. http://www.sandiegouniontribune.com/sdut-pokemon-go-encinitas-cliff-fall-2016jul13-story.html
12. Kerr, E.: Pokemon Go: police issue warning to gamers. BBC News, 17 July 2016. http://www.bbc.com/news/uk-northern-ireland-36818838
13. Kirman, B., Linehan, C., Lawson, S.: Blowtooth: a provocative pervasive game for smuggling virtual drugs through real airport security. Pers. Ubiquit. Comput. **16**(6), 767–775 (2012)
14. Linehan, C., Bull, N., Kirman, B.: BOLLOCKS!! Designing pervasive games that play with the social rules of built environments. In: Reidsma, D., Katayose, H., Nijholt, A. (eds.) ACE 2013. LNCS, vol. 8253, pp. 123–137. Springer, Cham (2013). https://doi.org/10.1007/978-3-319-03161-3_9

15. Linehan, C., Harrer, S., Kirman, B., Lawson, S., Carter, M.: Games against health: a player-centered design philosophy. In: Proceedings of the 33rd Annual ACM Conference Extended Abstracts on Human Factors in Computing Systems, pp. 589–600. ACM (2015)
16. Shove, E., Pantzar, M., Watson, M.: The Dynamics of Social Practice: Everyday Life and How It Changes. Sage publications, Thousand Oaks (2012)
17. Sobel, K., Bhattacharya, A., Hiniker, A., Lee, J.H., Kientz, J.A., Yip, J.C.: It wasn't really about the Pokémon: parents' perspectives on a location-based mobile game. In: Proceedings of CHI 2017, pp. 1483–1496. ACM (2017)

Beating the City: Three Inspirational Design Patterns to Promote Social Play Through Aligning Rhythms

Robb Mitchell[1(✉)] and Thomas Olsson[2]

[1] University of Southern Denmark, Kolding, Denmark
robb@sdu.dk
[2] Tampere University of Technology, Tampere, Finland

Abstract. This paper offers three inspirational design patterns for sparking social play between unacquainted people in public and semi-public spaces. The intention is to support developers in appreciating and articulating possible approaches in creating physical or digital artefacts as interventions that encourage unacquainted people to play together in urban areas. As part of a broader selection of design examples with such social effects, we present three inspirational design patterns related to the notion of *rhythm*: "Sharing Vibrations", "Actions That Need Another", and "Crosswire Outputs". Although the creators of our accompanying design examples did not explicitly propose them neither as games, nor urban interventions, we believe that they have strongly playable qualities that can help inspire opportunities to increase playability in unexpected moments in city places.

Keywords: Design patterns social interaction · Social play · Urban icebreakers

1 Introduction

To foster the hospitality and openness of a playable city [27] we propose that social play experiences are crucial as both ends and means. Playable cities have great potential to increase the sociality of cities for both residents and visitors. Shared playful interactions in urban environments may result in greater social cohesion, senses of belonging and community [14], and perceptions of welcome-ness. Thus, playable cities share many of the characteristics of other attempts to provoke more interpersonal contact between unacquainted people in public places. Increasing the likelihood of strangers interacting also increases the chances that they might play together. For a fresh perspective on facilitating co-located fun in our cities, playable city advocates might look towards a wide range of art and design experimentation specifically concerned with fostering new encounters between unacquainted people.

In many situations, play between people can be difficult because people feel inhibited for various reasons. The reasons vary from person to person, and from situation to situation; however, in general such "social boundaries" [28] can be said to originate from, for example, cultural norms, personality characteristics like shyness, lack of awareness of common ground with the other possible players, and the risk of being embarrassed. In this paper, we zoom in on three possible inhibitors of social interaction in public spaces and

© ICST Institute for Computer Sciences, Social Informatics and Telecommunications Engineering 2018
Y. Chisik et al. (Eds.): INTETAIN 2017, LNICST 215, pp. 159–163, 2018.
https://doi.org/10.1007/978-3-319-73062-2_15

present some simple advice and diverse examples as to how these barriers may be overcome. Practitioners and researchers from many fields have proposed a wide variety of interventions [26], gadgets [5, 25], installations [10], objects, and apparel [16] to support initiating interactions between co-located people). However, a systematically presented collection of existing social icebreaking design examples appears lacking. To address this, we have been conducting an ongoing design space review examining diverse examples of both high and low-tech efforts for sparking social interactions. Crucial to informing this design space investigation has been our facilitation of an international series of workshops in which interdisciplinary teams comparing and critiquing diverse examples of possible social icebreakers, drawn from many fields [19].

Our intention in developing inspirational design patterns is to provide stimulus rather than prescriptions. This is in the spirit of Jonas Löwgren's suggestion to "broaden the repertoire of the interaction design community" with *inspirational* patterns for embodied interaction [13]. We do not aim to provide an exhaustive taxonomy of all the possibilities for designers to facilitate playful interactions as the range of means by which technology may influence interpersonal encounters is potentially endless. We also do not intend to rank the effectiveness of different design strategies against each other in absolute terms, as contextual factors are hugely important for the success of any playful social catalyst design [2, 9]. Thus, similarly to influential notion of "strong concepts" for HCI [11] we make no claim at universality for our patterns. Also similar to strong concepts, successful use of inspirational design patterns requires skills and knowledge of particular contexts. The inspiration patterns offered follow a similar form but are different in scope and content to previously published other subsets of patterns that focus on proximity [18] and filtering of encounters [19].

Finally, this work complements the work of [23] in outlining the design space and design challenges for interactions between strangers. The examples we present to illustrate our design patterns are broader than only urban oriented. We nevertheless hope our focus on the fostering social encounters may be a useful complement to other descriptions of interventions concerned increasing the playability of cities [21] and related experimentation with pervasive gaming [6]. The inspirational patterns we offer may help foster informal social play in their own right, or can be social icebreakers that help facilitate more structured forms of collaborative play or multi-user games.

We draw upon Alexander's original format for presenting design patterns [1] in the following three subsections. We give each of our inspirational patterns a short name and after this (in italics) offer possible problem statement concerning initiating social interaction. Then we offer a one-line summary of a possible way to think about this challenge, before presenting two examples that illustrate each abstraction. After the pairs of design examples we offer a brief speculation concerning how each inspiration pattern might be applied in designing playful cities.

Sharing Vibrations

It is easy to ignore the presence of other people and not consider that our actions may effect them.

We argue that physical sensations that increase awareness about the presence of other people can also increase the chances of lightweight social interaction.

Gravicells by Seiko Mikami and Soto Ichiwaka (2004) is a digital installation that offers a simulation of the forces of gravity. Visitor movements are detected by floor based sensors that trigger audiovisual effects [3:23]. Most striking are the dynamic black and white ripples projected on the floor around each visitor. The presence of more than one person on the floor causes more complex patterns to be projected. This effect is somewhat akin to the intermeshing of radiating ripples on a pond when two thrown stones perturb the water surface at different points (author's personal observation).

Net Berlin by Numen (2013) is part of a series of gigantic multi-layered hammock-like installations. This iteration consisted of multiple levels of interconnected rope nets that invited visitors to explore by climbing and rolling, or simply lounging around [24:13]. Vigorous movements of visitors in non-digital installation caused vibrations that could be felt throughout the whole structure, and even gentle movements could be detected across and between different levels. This was because a portion of net that functioned as a floor for one participant, could simultaneously also be a ceiling or wall for another participant.

This pattern appears especially ripe for supporting the transition between parallel play and "interference play" [7, 15].

Actions That Need Another

Initiating interpersonal contact can be difficult without any practical reason.

Create opportunities and challenges that require assistance from another person to encourage collaboration.

SHARE by Stephanie Chen (2007) is a flattish box comprising four drawers for serving sushi. The four drawers all face in a different direction. A handle-like ribbon is attached to the front of every drawer. A mechanism inside the box prevents drawers being opened individually. To access the food requires two or more people pulling several ribbon-handles at the same time from different directions [4].

Friendly Twist by Coca Cola [20] was a set of bottle cap designs distributed by a soft drinks company as part of a promotional campaign. The cap of each bottle was designed so that it could interlock with the cap of other bottles in the campaign. Furthermore, the bottle was sealed very tight, so that it was only possible to unscrew the cap through dovetailing and twisting the cap of one person's bottle with another person's bottle.

We suggest the interdependency [12, 17] that this pattern exploits has potential for eliciting collaborative playfulness and can be considered for applying to playful designs that require not only instrumental use of hands, but almost any other sense-able body part, action or state.

Crosswire Outputs

It can be difficult to notice and appreciate the actions of another person.

Make the actions of one person appear as if they are done by another person in order to provide shared elements of surprise and bewilderment.

Remote Furniture by Fujimura (1999) is a pair of motorized, connected rocking chairs. Activity in either rocking chair is detected by movement sensors that cause actuators in the other chair to move a corresponding amount, thus creating a kind of echo, or mirror of rocking motors in the opposite chair [8].

Reversed Megaphone by Caspar Obrø and Mads Hobye (2011) is another pair of recognizable artefacts: namely two megaphones. The mic and loudspeakers of each megaphone are cross wired with each other so that audio inputs to one megaphone are transmitted to, and amplified by the other megaphone (and vice versa) [22]. When two people are using a megaphone each, a boisterous form of ventriloquism results.

In addition to provoking various forms of playing with identity, this pattern may also offer a route to many other kinds of shared amusement such as personal expression, teasing, pranks and turn taking games.

2   Conclusion

We have presented three design approaches (or *patterns*) that we hope can provoke designs for promoting social play between collocated strangers. The patterns build on the notion of mutual *rhythm* (i.e., coordinated and synchronized action) that would be created in physical and digital artefacts. The provided examples are part of a broader collection of designs that manifest various approaches to encouraging collective action and play between unacquainted people particularly in public spaces and urban areas.

References

1. Alexander, C.: A Pattern Language: Towns, Buildings, Construction. Oxford University Press, Oxford (1977)
2. Balestrini, M., Marshall, P., Cornejo, R., Tentori, M., Bird, J., Rogers, Y.: Jokebox: coordinating shared encounters in public spaces. In: Proceedings of the 19th ACM Conference on Computer-Supported Cooperative Work and Social Computing (CSCW 2016), pp. 38–49. ACM, New York (2016). https://doi.org/10.1145/2818048.2835203
3. Brouwer, J.: Feelings Are Always Local. V2_Publishing, Rotterdam (2004)
4. Chen, S.: SHARE: interactive food packaging (2007). http://chendesignlab.com/designresearch/share/. Accessed 21 May 2017
5. Donath, J.: The Social Machine: Designs for Living Online. MIT Press, Cambridge (2014)
6. Duggan, E.: Squaring the (magic) circle: a brief definition and history of pervasive games. In: Nijholt, A. (ed.) Playable Cities. GMSE, pp. 111–135. Springer, Singapore (2017). https://doi.org/10.1007/978-981-10-1962-3_6
7. Frost, J.L., Wortham, S.C., Reifel, R.S.: Play and Child Development. Pearson/Merrill Prentice Hall, Upper Saddle River (2008)
8. Fujimura, N.: Remote furniture: interactive art installation for public space. In: Elliott-Famularo, H. (ed.) ACM SIGGRAPH 2004 Emerging technologies (SIGGRAPH 2004). ACM, New York (2004). https://doi.org/10.1145/1186155.1186179
9. Heinemann, T., Mitchell, R.: Breaching barriers to collaboration in public spaces. In: Proceedings of the 8th International Conference on Tangible, Embedded and Embodied Interaction (TEI 2014), pp. 213–220. ACM, New York (2004). https://doi.org/10.1145/2540930.2540951
10. Hespanhol, L., Dalsgaard, P.: Social interaction design patterns for urban media architecture. In: Abascal, J., Barbosa, S., Fetter, M., Gross, T., Palanque, P., Winckler, M. (eds.) INTERACT 2015. LNCS, vol. 9298, pp. 596–613. Springer, Cham (2015). https://doi.org/10.1007/978-3-319-22698-9_41

11. Höök, K., Löwgren, J.: Strong concepts: intermediate-level knowledge in interaction design research. ACM Trans. Comput. Hum. Interact. **19**(3), 18 (2012). https://doi.org/10.1145/2362364.2362371. Article no. 23
12. Isbister, K., Abe, K., Karlesky, M.: Interdependent wearables (for play): a strong concept for design. In: Proceedings of the 2017 CHI Conference on Human Factors in Computing Systems (CHI 2017), pp. 465–471. ACM (2017). https://doi.org/10.1145/3025453.3025939
13. Löwgren, J.: Inspirational patterns for embodied interaction. Knowl. Technol. Policy **20**(3), 165–177 (2007)
14. McMillan, D.W., Chavis, D.M.: Sense of community: a definition and theory. J. Community Psychol. **14**(1), 6–23 (1986)
15. Marshall, J., Benford, S., Pijnappel, S.: Expanding exertion gaming. Int. J. Hum.-Comput. Stud. **90**, 1–13 (2016)
16. Mitchell, R.: Sensing mine, yours, theirs, and ours: interpersonal ubiquitous interactions. In: Adjunct Proceedings of the 2015 ACM International Joint Conference on Pervasive and Ubiquitous Computing and Proceedings of the 2015 ACM International Symposium on Wearable Computers (UbiComp/ISWC 2015 Adjunct), pp. 933–938. ACM, New York (2015). https://doi.org/10.1145/2800835.2806203
17. Mitchell, R., Bravo, C.S.B., Skouby, A.H., Möller, R.L.: Blind running: perceptual team interdependency for self-less play. In: Proceedings of the 2015 Annual Symposium on Computer-Human Interaction in Play (CHI PLAY 2015), pp. 649–654. ACM, New York (2015). https://doi.org/10.1145/2793107.2810308
18. Mitchell, R., Boer, L.: Move closer: towards design patterns to support initiating social encounters. In: Proceedings of the 2017 CHI Conference Extended Abstracts on Human Factors in Computing Systems (CHI EA 2017), pp. 2781–2787. ACM, New York (2015). https://doi.org/10.1145/3027063.3053230
19. Mitchell, R., Olsson, T.: Barriers for bridging interpersonal gaps: three inspirational design patterns for increasing collocated social interaction In: Proceedings of the 8th International Conference on Communities and Technologies. ACM (2017)
20. Monloss, K.: Ad of the Day: Coke Designs a Friendly Bottle That Can Only Be Opened by Another Bottle. AdWeek (2014). Accessed 21 May 2017
21. Nijholt, A.: Towards playful and playable cities. In: Nijholt, A. (ed.) Playable Cities. GMSE, pp. 1–20. Springer, Singapore (2017). https://doi.org/10.1007/978-981-10-1962-3_1
22. Obrø, C., Hobye, M.: Reversed Megaphone (2014). www.hobye.dk/projects/megaphone. Accessed 21 May 2017
23. Paasovaara, S., Lucero, A., Olsson, T.: Outlining the design space of playful interactions between nearby strangers. In: Proceedings of the 20th International Academic Mindtrek Conference (AcademicMindtrek 2016), pp. 216–225. ACM, New York (2016). https://doi.org/10.1145/2994310.2994344
24. Schneiderman, D., Winton, A.G.: Textile Technology and Design: From Interior Space to Outer Space. Bloomsbury Publishing, London (2016)
25. Paulos, E., Goodman, E.: The familiar stranger: anxiety, comfort, and play in public places. In: Proceedings of the SIGCHI Conference on Human Factors in Computing Systems (CHI 2004), pp. 223–230. ACM, New York (2004). https://doi.org/10.1145/985692.985721
26. Todd, C., Scordelis, A.: Causing a Scene. Harper Collins, New York (2009)
27. Watershed Call for Proposals—Making the City Playable Conference—Watershed, Bristol, UK, 10–11 September 2014 (2014)
28. Wirth, L.: Urbanism as a way of life. Am. J. Sociol. **44**, 1–24 (2014)

Author Index

Printed in the United States
By Bookmasters